JUDICIAL REVIEW AND COMPLIANCE WITH ADMINISTRATIVE LAW

How effective is judicial review in securing compliance with administrative law? This book presents an empirically-based study of the influence of judicial review on government agencies. In doing so, it explores judicial review from a regulatory perspective and uses the insights of the regulation literature to reflect on the capacity of judicial review to modify government behaviour. On the basis of extensive research with heavily litigated government agencies, the book develops a framework for analysing and researching the regulatory capacity of judicial review. Combining empirical and legal analysis, it describes the conditions which must exist to maximise judicial review's capacity to secure compliance with administrative law.

The book will be essential reading for anyone interested in judicial review and administrative law.

Judicial Review and Compliance with Administrative Law

SIMON HALLIDAY

Nicholas de B Katzenbach Research Fellow
Centre for Socio-Legal Studies, Oxford University

·HART·
PUBLISHING
OXFORD AND PORTLAND, OREGON
2004

Published in North America (US and Canada) by
Hart Publishing
c/o International Specialized Book Services
5804 NE Hassalo Street
Portland, Oregon
97213–3644
USA

Hart Publishing is a specialist legal publisher based in Oxford, England. To order further copies of this book or to request a list of other publications please write to:

Hart Publishing, Salters Boatyard, Folly Bridge, Abingdon Rd, Oxford, OX1 4LB
Telephone: +44 (0)1865 245533 Fax: +44 (0) 1865 794882
email: mail@hartpub.co.uk
WEBSITE: http//:www.hartpub.co.uk

British Library Cataloguing in Publication Data
Data Available

ISBN 1–84113–265–9 (hardback)

Typeset by Hope Services, Abingdon
Printed and bound in Great Britain by
MPG Books Ltd, Bodmin, Cornwall

For Mark

Acknowledgements

This book began its life as my PhD thesis at Strathclyde University's Law School (though it has changed much since then). All the people I thanked in the thesis are due thanks again now, particularly the local authorities which took part in the research. A second mention should also be made of my supervisors Neil Hutton and Peter Robson, and of Cyrus Tata, all of whom were very encouraging and helpful right from the start (when it was much needed).

I have been very fortunate to have been able to use research fellowships at the Centre for Socio-Legal Studies and at Balliol College, Oxford University, to pursue a number of research projects, including this one. I am very grateful to Denis Galligan and my colleagues here at the Centre, and to the Master and Fellows of Balliol for providing an environment where I was given substantial freedom to pursue my research while at the same time enjoying the considerable practical and moral support of my colleagues and the institutions themselves.

Some of the work on this book was developed while a visiting scholar at the Law School of the University of New South Wales. I am grateful to Jill McKeough and her colleagues for the provision of research facilities and the warmth of their welcome. During that I time I benefited from discussions with Brendan Edgeworth, Arthur Glass, Martin Krygier and Christine Parker in particular. Other friends and colleagues have been of notable assistance during the life of this project. Tania Boyt, our tireless administrator at the Centre, took time away from her many tasks to draw the diagram summarising the analytical framework in chapter 9. Chas Gay, Brent Plate and Melisa Rodriguez provided the substance on more than one occasion when inspiration for working on the PhD and book was needed. Mike Adler has been very generous in being enthusiastic about this book and in offering much valued advice and feedback. Thanks are also due to Liora Lazarus and Karen Yeung who have been a great support in many ways throughout the writing of the text, but in particular to Karen Yeung who read a few of the chapters in draft and sharpened my thinking about regulatory perspectives (though not sufficiently in her view, I suspect). I am especially indebted to Bronwen Morgan who went considerably beyond the call of duty and friendship and read the whole manuscript. She offered characteristically insightful and carefully pitched suggestions and the book has improved as a result.

Finally, I would like to thank Richard Hart, April Boffin and the team at Hart Publishing for their encouragement and patience and for being such a lovely group of people to work with.

Simon Halliday
Oxford, October 2003

Contents

Table of Cases   xv

PART ONE: INTRODUCTION

1: *The Enquiry*   3

OVERVIEW OF JUDICIAL REVIEW IMPACT RESEARCH   5
The Scope of this Enquiry   6
What Do We Mean by 'Administrative Law'?   8
Judicial Impact and the Limits of a Compliance Focus   9
**Bottom-up and Top-down Approaches and the Great
Methodological Divide**   9
PLACING THE INFLUENCE OF JUDICIAL REVIEW IN REGULATORY
PERSPECTIVE   10
Why 'Regulation'?   10
Regulatory Standards and Regulatory Goals   11
The Regulatory Goal of Administrative Law   12
Two Levels of a 'Regulatory Perspective'   14
The Various Functions of Judicial Review   15
The Heuristic Device   16
What is the Level of Optimal Compliance?   16
*Is Perfect Compliance the Regulatory Goal of Judicial
Review?*   17
Weight of Individual Conditions   17
Questions of Degree   18
RESEARCH METHODS   19
Research Approach   19
Research Techniques   20
Choice of Research Subjects   21
Timbergreens   23
Muirfield   25
Eastbank   26
AN OVERVIEW OF HOMELESSNESS LAW   28
The Homeless Persons' Obstacle Race   29

Homelessness	29
Priority Need	30
Intentionality	30
Local Connection	30
Legislative Changes During Fieldwork	31
A BRIEF OVERVIEW OF THE BOOK	31
Part 2: The Decision-Makers	32
Part 3: The Decision-Making Environment	33
Part 4: The Law	34
Part 5: Conclusion	35

PART 2: THE DECISION-MAKERS

2: *The Reception of Legal Knowledge into Government Agencies*	39
THE COMPLEXITY OF ORGANISATIONS AND ITS IMPLICATIONS FOR THE RECEPTION OF LEGAL KNOWLEDGE	41
Structure and Operations of Muirfield Council's Homeless Persons Unit	41
Casework Team	42
Assessments and Advice Team	43
Temporary Accommodation Team	44
Implications for the Reception of Legal Knowledge	45
BARRIERS TO KNOWLEDGE DISSEMINATION	46
Organisational Complexity and the Containment of Legal Knowledge	46
Relationships with Legal Advisors	50
3: *Legal Conscientiousness*	53
PROFESSIONAL INTUITION	54
CULTURE OF SUSPICION	55
Understanding a Culture of Suspicion	59
CREATIVE COMPLIANCE AND A LACK OF FAITH IN LAW	60
Lacking Faith in Law to Produce the Right Decision	60
Avoiding Legal Control	61
Abusing Legal Process	61
Bullet Proofing Decisions	63
Pre-empting the Creative Tactics of 'Bogus' Applicants	64

THE RELATIONSHIP BETWEEN LEGAL CONSCIENTIOUSNESS AND
LEGAL KNOWLEDGE   65

CONCLUSION   68

4: *Legal Competence*   71

RELATIONAL DISTANCE BETWEEN THE COURTS AND THE
ADMINISTRATION   72

Interpretive Communities and Compliance   72

BUREAUCRATIC APPLICATION OF LEGAL KNOWLEDGE   74

Case Study of Timbergreens   74

The Spirit and Letter of Administrative Law   80

BOUNDED APPLICATION OF LEGAL KNOWLEDGE   80

CONCLUSION   82

PART 3: THE DECISION-MAKING ENVIRONMENT

5: *The Decision-Making Environment*   87

INTRODUCTION   87

THE PLURALITY OF NORMATIVE SYSTEMS WITHIN THE
DECISION-MAKING ENVIRONMENT   88

Financial Management   89
*Case Study of Eastbank and Temporary Accommodation
Pressures*   89
Conclusion   93

Performance Audit   94
Case Study of Muirfield and Performance Related Pay   94
Conclusion   96

Political Pressure   96
*Case Study of Muirfield and Local Political Antipathy
Towards the Homeless*   97
Conclusion   99

More Remote Social/Political Features   99

WHAT CONDITIONS LAW'S STRENGTH IN THE ENVIRONMENT?   101

The Role of Sanctions   103

Persuasion   105

Flexibility   106

CONCLUSION   106

PART 4: THE LAW

6: *The Contestedness of Administrative Justice*   111

ADMINISTRATIVE JUSTICE SCHOLARSHIP   113
Administrative Justice and Administrative Legality   113
What Activities are Covered by 'Administrative Justice'?   114
Different Treatments of Administrative Justice in
Socio-Legal Scholarship   114
CONCEPTIONS OF ADMINISTRATIVE JUSTICE   116
Mashaw's Models of Administrative Justice   116
Developments on Mashaw   119
The Significance of the Professional Treatment Model   119
The Exhaustiveness of Mashaw's Typology   120
Discussion of Adler's Development of Mashaw   121
CONCLUSION   124

7: *Judicial Control and Agency Autonomy*   127

INTRODUCTION   127
The Study of Administrative Law   128
COMPETITION BETWEEN JUDICIAL CONTROL AND AGENCY
AUTONOMY   130
Introduction   130
Substantive Rationality of Decision-Outcomes   132
Unreasonableness   132
Disproportionality   136
Error of Law   137
Questions of Fact and Law   139
Rationality of Decision-Making Process   142
Statutory Requirements about Fact-Finding   142
CONCLUSION   143

8: *The Competition between Individual and Agency Interests*   145

PROCEDURAL FAIRNESS   145
Administrative Efficiency   147
National Security   149
RATIONALITY OF DECISION-MAKING PROCESS   150
Administrative Policies   150
Relevant and Irrelevant Facts   153

CONCLUSION TO PART 4   156

PART 5: CONCLUSION

9: *Judicial Review and Compliance with Administrative Law*   161

    INTRODUCTION   161

    THE ANALYTICAL APPROACH OF THIS BOOK   162

    Typologies of Decision-Makers   162

    Continuums of Conditions Affecting Compliance   164

    The Decision-Makers   164

    The Decision-Making Environment   165

    The Law   165

    APPLYING THE FRAMEWORK BEYOND THE CONTEXT OF
HOMELESSNESS ADMINISTRATION   166

    Introduction   166

    **Varying Significance of Legal Conscientiousness
According to Context**   169

    *Legal Conscientiousness and Homelessness
Administration*   169

    *Would Legal Conscientiousness be as Important in Other
Contexts?*   171

    **Conclusions about Applying the Framework to Other
Contexts**   173

    FUTURE ENQUIRY   174

Bibliography   177

Index   185

Table of Cases

Anisminic Ltd v Foreign Compensation Commission
  [1969] 2 AC 147 137
Associated Provincial Picture Houses Ltd v Wednesbury
  Corporation [1948] 1 KB 223 ....129, 130, 133–5,
                                             136, 137, 141, 153, 158
Attorney General v Ryan [1980] AC 718 146
Attorney General ex rel Tilley v Wandsworth LBC [1981]
  1 WLR 854...151
Begum v London Borough of Tower Hamlets [2003]
  2 WLR 388...148
Board of Education v Rice [1911] AC 179 146–7
British Oxygen Co Ltd v Board of Trade [1971] AC 610 152
Council for Civil Service Unions v Minister for the Civil Service
  [1985] AC 374 ....128, 132, 133, 136, 138, 149
Credit Suisse v Allerdale M.B.C. [1997] QB 306.............................138
Credit Suisse v Waltham Forest LBC [1997] QB 362 138
D and J Nicol v Dundee Harbour Trustees 1915 SC (HL) 7...........129
Edwards v Bairstow [1956] AC 14 140
Elliott v Brighton BC (1980) 79 LGR 506 151
Errington v Minister of Health [1935] 1 KB 249 148
Express and Star Ltd v Bunday [1988] ICR 379 141
Farmer v Cotton's Trustees [1915] AC 922 130
Hall & Co Ltd v Shoreham-by-Sea Urban District Council [1964]
  1 WLR 240...133
H Lavender & Sons v Minister of Housing and Local Government
  [1970] 1 WLR 1231..151
Inland Revenue Comrs v Hood Barrs 1961 SC (HL) 22 146
Kanda v Malaya [1962] AC 322...146
Kilmarnock Magistrates v Secretary of State for Scotland
  1961 SC 350 151
Lloyd v McMahon [1987] AC 625 ....145, 147
Local Government Board v Arlidge [1915] AC 120..........................148
London and Clydeside Estates Ltd v Aberdeen District Council
  1980 SC (HL) 1 129

London and Midland Developments v Secretary of State for
  Scotland 1996 SCLR 465...154
McCallum v Arthur 1955 SC 188...151
McColl v Strathclyde Regional Council 1983 SLT 616 138
Padfield v Minister of Agriculture, Fisheries and Food
  [1968] AC 997 154
Quiltotex Co Ltd v Minister of Housing and Local Government
  and Another [1966] 1 QB 704 139
R v Barnet LBC ex parte Shah [1983] 2 AC 309...............................139
R v Barnsley JJ, ex parte Barnsley & District Licensed Victualler's
  Association [1960] 2 QB 167 147
R v Cambridge Health Authority ex parte B [1995] 1 WLR 898......155
R v Chief Constable of Sussex ex parte International Trader's
  Ferry Ltd [1999] 2 AC 418.....................................134, 137, 154, 155
R v Civil Services Appeal Board ex parte Cunningham [1991]
  4 All ER 310..146
R v East Sussex County Court ex parte Tandy [1998]
  AC 714...153, 155–6
R v Gloucestershire County Council ex parte Barry [1997]
  AC 584 ....154, 156
R v Higher Education Funding Council ex parte the Institute of
  Dental Surgery [1994] 1 All ER 651...146
R v Hillingdon LBC ex parte Puhlhofer [1986]
  1 AC 484...140, 141
R v Home Secretary ex parte Doody [1994] AC 531.................145, 146
R v Home Secretary ex parte Venables [1998] AC 407
R v Housing Appeal Tribunal [1920] 3 KB 334 147
R v Hull University Visitor ex parte Page [1993]
  AC 682 ....137, 138, 139
R v Industrial Injuries Commissioner ex parte Amalgamated
  Engineering Union (No 2) [1966] 2 QB 31 141
R v Inland Revenue Commissioners ex parte national Federation of
  Self-Employed and Small Businesses Ltd [1982] AC 617 136
R v Leicestershire Fire Authority ex parte Thompson (1978)
  77 LGR 373..146
R v London Borough of Tower Hamlets ex parte Hoque,
  The Times, 20 July 1993..142
R v London County Council ex parte Corrie [1981] 1 KB 68 151
R v Minister of Defence ex parte Murray [1998] COD 134............146
R v Minister of Defence ex parte Smith [1996] QB 517....................135

R v Port of London Authority ex parte Kynoch Ltd [1919]
1 KB 176 ....151, 152

R v Rotherham Licensing JJ ex parte Chapman [1939]
2 All ER 710 151

R v Royal Borough of Kensington and Chelsea ex parte Bayani
22 HLR 406 142–3

R v Secretary of State for the Environment ex parte Hatton BC
(1983) LGR 662 151

R v Secretary of State for the Environment ex parte Kirkstall
Valley Campaign Ltd [1996] 3 All ER 304 146

R v Secretary of State for Health, ex parte US Tobacco International
Inc [1992] QB 353 147

R v Secretary of State for the Home Department ex parte Al-Fayed
(No.1) [1998] 1 WLR 763 146

R v Secretary of State for the Home Department ex parte
Brind [1991] 1 AC 696 ....135, 136

R v Secretary of State for the Home Department ex parte
Cheblak [1991] 2 All ER 319 150

R v Secretary of State for the Home Department ex parte
Hosenball [1977] 3 All ER 452 150

R v Somerset CC ex parte Fewings [1995] 1 WLR 1037 138

R v Sussex JJ ex parte McCarthy [1924] 1 KB 256 147

R (on the Application of Alconbury Developments Ltd) v Secretary
of State for Environment, Transport and the Regions [2001]
HRLR 45 ....137, 148

R (on the application of Wulfsohn) v Legal Services Commission
[2001] EWHC Admin 409 134

Ransom v Higgs [1974] 1 WLR 1594 140

Ridge v Baldwin [1964] AC 40 ....146, 148

Russell v Duke of Norfolk [1949] 1 All ER 109 145

Secretary of State for Education and Science v Tameside
Metropolitan Borough Council [1977] AC 1014 134

South Oxfordshire District Council v Secretary of State for the
Environment [1981] 1 WLR 1092 154

Stringer v Minister of Housing and Local Government [1970]
1 WLR 1281 151

Tesco Stores Ltd v Secretary of State for the Environment
[1995] 1 WLR 759 154

Watt v Lord Advocate 1979 SC 120 138

West v Secretary of State for Scotland 1992 SC 385 136

West Glamorgan County Council v Rafferty [1987] 1 WLR 457.....134
Wilson v Nithsdale SLT 1992 113..153
Wilson v Secretary of State for Environment [1973] 1 WLR 1083 ...147
Wiseman v Borneman [1971] AC 297 148
Woodhouse v Brotherhood Ltd [1972] QB 520..............................139
Young v Criminal Injuries Compensation Board 1997 SLT 297 147

Part 1: Introduction

1

The Enquiry

THIS BOOK IS about the relationship between judicial and administrative decision-making. Its aim is to set out a framework for
thinking about the extent to which judicial review litigation influences
administrative behaviour and is capable of securing compliance with
the requirements of administrative law (as expounded through judicial
review). This work has emerged from an empirical investigation of
routine local government decision-making (administering English
homelessness law). The analytical framework presented in this book,
accordingly, is rooted in a sociological understanding of how these
agencies worked, how they understood law and their experiences of
judicial review, and the significance of those understandings to their
daily, routine (and often mundane) working practices.

   The book sits comfortably within an emerging body of work within
UK administrative law scholarship which explores the impact of judicial review on administrative behaviour. However, the approach taken
here avoids the attempt to describe the 'impact' of judicial review on
the government agencies[1] which took part in the study. The task of
linking cause and effect in tracing the relationship between judicial
review and administrative behaviour is fraught with difficulty at both
a micro (Halliday, 1998; Sunkin, 2004) and macro level (Schultz and
Gottlieb, 1998). How does one isolate, for example, the influence of
judicial review from among the many, at times chaotic, pressures
within the administrative arena? Further, even if one manages such a
task, when does one give up in tracking the impact? These kinds of
questions illustrate the considerable difficulty involved in trying to
capture the 'impact' of judicial review. Accordingly, an alternative
approach is taken in this book: it is to speculate about the conditions

---

[1] Throughout this book I use the term ' government agency' to refer, fairly loosely, to
a public sector respondent body's decision-making unit. The term is not intended to
confer any precise meaning, but is rather referring to a government organisation which
makes decisions—including local government bodies. 'Agency', then, may refer to
central government departments, as well as local government organisations, as well as
various sub-units within such organisations.

and factors which mediate the influence of judicial review judgments on administrative behaviour. Or, to put it another way, this books sets out to explore the barriers to judicial review's influence over the administration. Most of these barriers relate to the decision-makers within government and the environment in which they work. Some of the barriers, however, relate to the nature of administrative law.

The analysis in this book, accordingly, emerges from a combination of the micro-sociological study of local government administration and a legal analysis of administrative law. Such a blend of sociological and doctrinal concerns allows us to build a framework for hypothesising about whether and to what extent judicial review may secure compliance with administrative law. Neither the doctrinal study of administrative law, nor the sociological study of administration in isolation is sufficient to tell us enough about the relationship between the two. The approach adopted in this book should not only offer deeper insights into the relationship between judicial review and administrative decision-making, it will also provide a framework for taking the research agenda forward. The book's analysis is structured around a series of hypotheses about the conditions which are significant to whether (and the extent to which) compliance with administrative law can be secured through judicial review. The more these conditions are in existence, the stronger compliance with administrative law will be. The less they are present, the weaker compliance will be. Such a series of hypotheses may be tested in future research, and insights accordingly refined, in a variety of administrative contexts. Slowly and systematically, then, a more detailed and comprehensive picture can be constructed of judicial review's capacity as a regulator of administrative behaviour. Although it has almost become trite in the developing body of empirical work to bemoan the lack of empirical evidence on the question of judicial review's influence (Richardson, 2004), the claim is still a powerful one and will remain so for some time to come. The research agenda is broad, and is therefore demanding for those who take up the challenge. It is hoped that the thesis of this book will help to set the stage for, and encourage, further enquiry.

The aims of this opening chapter are fivefold: first, to situate this work within the emerging field in UK administrative law scholarship which focuses on the impact of judicial review; secondly, to discuss in detail the basic approach of this study—the placing of the impact of judicial review in a regulatory perspective; thirdly, to describe the research methods used to collect the empirical data; fourthly, to offer a very basic overview of homelessness law; and finally, to give a snapshot of the thesis of the book as a whole.

OVERVIEW OF JUDICIAL REVIEW IMPACT RESEARCH

The UK scholarship on the impact of judicial review has recently been summarised and analysed by Richardson (2004). Some of the details of the findings of these studies are discussed and referred to when the empirical data from this study is presented in the chapters which follow. This section, then, will not attempt to summarise the findings of previous research. However, a few words here are nevertheless merited in order to offer at the outset a sense of the body of work which is emerging in the UK and of the kind of research questions that are being asked. This will help us see the range of research which can be conducted in this field, and the distinctiveness of the approach taken in this book.

At one level, there is work which, from an external perspective, draws an inference about the role of judicial review cases in provoking executive reactions in terms of legislative, or policy developments (Harlow, 1976; Prosser, 1983; Loughlin and Quinn, 1993; Richardson, 1993; Livingstone, 1995; Thomas, 2003). Much of this kind of work is close to the concerns of the law and courts sub-field of (mainly US) political science which seeks to assess the significance of the courts to social and political change (see, for example, Rosenberg, 1991; Schultz, 1998; Feeley and Rubin, 1999; Stone Sweet, 2000; Shapiro and Stone Sweet, 2002). The focus here is broadly on the macro level, and is concerned with the dynamics of power within the polity. Recent constitutional developments in the UK, particularly the Human Rights Act 1998, is likely to (or certainly should) make this kind of work more prevalent within UK socio-legal studies.

At another level there is a collection of empirical studies which have used a range of research techniques to penetrate the organisational culture of particular government agencies and to assess from the inside the impact of judicial review on decision-making processes (Bridges *et al.*, 1987; Sunkin and Le Sueur, 1991; Mullen, Pick and Prosser, 1996; Obadina, 1998; Halliday, 2000a; Richardson and Machin, 2000; Sunkin and Pick, 2001). The focus here is more at the micro level and the concern has been to test the power of the court to control administrative action, and/or to protect the rights of citizens as the subject of the state. Although related to the first group of studies, this second group is perhaps of a more specifically 'administrative law' flavour. Allied to this second group are a number of studies which, although of much the same vein, have used personal professional experience inside government agencies to reflect on the impact of judicial review on decision-making culture (Kerry, 1986; James, 1996; Hammond, 1998; Buck, 1998). Additionally, there is work which considers the impact of judicial review as part of much wider empirical projects (Loveland, 1995; Daintith and Page, 1999), and work which reflects on empirical research to consider the conditions under which judicial review will impact on agencies (Baldwin and McCrudden, 1987: chapter 4; Galligan, 2001).

Even this crude division of existing UK work into these groups illustrates the importance of being clear about what function one is ascribing to judicial review when trying to assess its impact or effectiveness. This point has been made persuasively by Cane (2004), where, in an international context, he suggests different models of judicial review, each with their own set of research questions about its 'impact'. However, even within a domestic context like England and Wales (the subject of the research which underpins this study), it is important to be clear about precisely which of judicial review's potential functions is the focus of the research endeavour. As Richardson and Sunkin (1996) have pointed out, research about the relationship between judicial review and administrative decision-making needs to be clear about what kinds of questions are being asked.

The Scope of this Enquiry

To this end, let me be clear about the scope of the enquiry. First, the thesis is rooted in a study of the routine decision-making practices of local authority housing departments in implementing English homelessness law (described in greater detail below). Although the wider ramifications of the research will be considered in the concluding chapter, the influence of judicial review is related in the first instance, through the presentation of the case study, to a particular form of government activity—what Galligan has called 'individualised, adjudicative decisions' (1986: 237):

> Here decisions are made by the application of standards which require a greater degree of enquiry and judgment, even discretion, than is provided by

routine administration [where the decision criteria are clear and precise and the facts are clear and uncontested], but fall short of strong policy-based discretion . . . In each case, the decision is made by an enquiry into the facts and a judgment applying authoritative standards to them. (1986: 236)

Secondly, unlike work such as that of Creyke and McMillan (2004) or Mullen, Pick and Prosser (1996),[2] my concern is not with the plight of the individual citizen consequent to judicial review. My focus is more future-oriented and relates to the ongoing activities of government agencies and the values which infuse their routine decisions. Nor is the focus on major policy or legislative developments in the vein of Prosser's classic study (1983) of the mobilisation of law through judicial review within the field of social welfare, and the reactions of government to this test case strategy (see also more generally Harlow and Rawlings, 1992). Rather, my objective is to offer an analytical framework which will be useful in thinking about and researching the effectiveness of judicial review as a regulatory mechanism in relation to the administrative decision-making practices of government agencies.

This is not to suggest, of course, that the sole function of judicial review is to promote compliance with administrative law by relevant government decision-makers. The various functions ascribed to judicial review need not be mutually exclusive. It has already been noted that researchers may also focus on the impact of litigation on the outcome of the particular governmental decision that gave rise to the judicial review action. Indeed, some scholars place a stress on the dispute resolution function of judicial review (see, for example, Pollard, 1998). Additionally, of course, one might see the role of judicial review in non-instrumental terms—as expressing appropriate political and moral values, regardless of whether respondents or other government decision-makers internalise them. Cane's concerns (2004), for example, about the scale and complexity of the empirical questions surrounding the influence of judicial review seem to push him towards the refuge of the expressive function of judicial review (where, admittedly, one can be reasonably confident that academic and policy debates might rest on fairly comprehensive foundations). The focus of this book on judicial review's ability to modify the decision-making behaviour of government decision-makers—its capacity as a regulator of government behaviour—is not intended to obscure or deny the additional functions

---

[2] Mullen et al's work, it should be noted, was broader in its aims than the focus on the plight of individual petitioners.

of judicial review. Nevertheless, it is being explored in isolation as a discrete enquiry. But this is simply one of the limits of this enquiry (which are inevitable and about which one should try to be explicit). We will return to this point briefly below.

What Do We Mean by 'Administrative Law'?

Another important question to be addressed in this opening chapter is what we mean by 'administrative law'. Harlow and Rawlings note that there are two different senses in which the term 'administrative law' might be used (1997: 72). It might be used to refer to the common law principles which police the lawfulness of government behaviour. Alternatively, it might be used to refer to the law of the administration—the substantive powers and duties of public agencies. The term is used here to encompass both senses. This study is organised around the question of the extent to which judicial review is effective in modifying government behaviour towards compliance with legality. In reviewing government decisions, the courts may apply the common law principles of administrative law, but they may also consider agencies' compliance with statutory duties—both procedural and substantive. Accordingly, this study considers the ability of judicial review to modify behaviour in line with legal requirements, regardless of whether they are based in the common law, or in the specific requirements of the statutory scheme being applied by the government agency. When the empirical data from this study is discussed later in the book, it will be clear that in addition to thinking about the common law principles of administrative law, the research also addresses the question of the extent to which judicial review was effective in securing compliance with the statutory scheme of social policy being implemented—English homelessness law. Although from an external perspective, the distinction between the two senses of administrative law may be helpful or significant, from the internal perspective of the administrative decision-makers, the distinction is less important. Common law and statutory duties all fall under the same umbrella of the legal demands that are made of them in performing their functions. It would, accordingly, be misleading to separate out the two senses for empirical analysis. And, significantly, as we shall see, the analytical framework for thinking about compliance with judicial mandates in the round is equally applicable to both senses of 'administrative law'.

Judicial Impact and the Limits of a Compliance Focus

Another point to be made which further refines the boundaries of this study concerns the significance of studying compliance with court rulings to the broader project of understanding the 'impact' of the courts on society—a traditional concern of political science 'judicial impact' studies (see Canon, 2004). The publication of Gerald Rosenberg's important book *The Hollow Hope* (1993) prompted considerable (though not necessarily new) critique concerning the limits of a 'court-centred' or 'top down' study of judicial impact, most notably from Michael McCann (1992; 1994). The argument runs, in summary, that to set oneself the task of assessing the power of the courts to secure compliance with its rulings is to engage in too narrow an enquiry which fails to observe or consider law's indirect and constitutive effects. Court rulings, in short, have a much wider role to play in society than to simply secure compliance with their narrow terms. They may be inspirational, providing a catalyst for social movements, or may be used as resources in situations of social conflict. They might be significant to ordinary people's shifting senses of value, identity and possibility, and so forth. All of this, it is suggested, is true and worthy of continued research endeavours. But it is not the subject of this enquiry. My aim is to study the influence of judicial review judgments on the bureaucracies which were subject to them, and to construct a framework out of this which can help us think about the ability of judicial review to positively influence bureaucratic processes. The broader significance and role of judicial review in society is explicitly excluded from the analysis. It should now be abundantly clear from this introductory section that there is a host of socio-legal questions to ask about the relationship between judicial review and social change. This study explores only one (though, it is suggested, indispensable) such question. This is bad news for readers who find other questions more interesting (though good news for researchers who are interested in pursuing the broader research enterprise).

Bottom-up and Top-down Approaches and the Great Methodological Divide

It is appropriate to note also at this stage that the debate between Rosenberg and McCann (McCann, 1992; Rosenberg 1996) speaks to a methodological divide between positivism and interpretivism in researching courts and social impact. McCann labels himself as an interpretivist conducting 'bottom-up' or 'de-centred' research about law's role in society. Rosenberg, on the other hand, labels himself as a positivist conducting 'top-down' or 'court-centred' research about the ability of the courts to produce social change. It is important to note (as does Sunkin, 2004), however, that these two sets of categories do not match perfectly. Insofar as labels are helpful (and often they are not, obscuring more than they reveal) I would label myself as an interpretivist conducting a court-centred research project. It is possible, in other words, to adopt an interpretivist approach to the study of compliance with judicial rulings. Given the fact that this study is focused on judicial review judgments and compliance with administrative law, it could easily be labelled as falling within the 'court-centred' camp. However, it adopts an explicitly interpretivist approach to investigating the significance of administrative law and judicial review to bureaucratic behaviour. The focus of this study on judicial review and compliance with administrative law is admittedly narrow and limited in what it can tell us about the courts' broader role in society, but the approach to understanding the relationship between judicial and administrative decision-making is interpretive

The methodological approach of this study is outlined in greater detail below. First, however, a few explanatory notes should be offered about placing the influence of judicial review in 'regulatory perspective'.

PLACING THE INFLUENCE OF JUDICIAL REVIEW IN REGULATORY PERSPECTIVE

A few important points of clarification need to be made if one is to explore the influence of judicial review in 'regulatory perspective'.

Why 'Regulation'?

The first question to be addressed is 'why talk about judicial review litigation in terms of regulation?'. Regulation is often used to refer to a technique of modern government whereby control is exercised (often through specialised agencies) over various aspects of social and economic life such as trade and commercial activity (for example, Kagan, 1978; McBarnet and Whelan, 1991; Black, 1997; Parker, 1999a), health and safety (for example, Baldwin, 1995; Hutter, 1997; Hawkins 2002), and the environment (for example, Richardson, Ogus and Burrows, 1983; Hawkins, 1984; Kagan, Gunningham and Thornton, 2003). It is also used to explore parallel processes of controlling activities *within* government (Hood, et al, 1999). Particular interest in 'regulation' has been sparked in part by privatisation of public utilities and their monitoring by newly created agencies (Baldwin and McCrudden, 1987; Hall, Scott and Hood, 2000). As such, regulation is usually seen as a discrete and identifiable form of governmental activity (Baldwin, Scott and Hood, 1998). To talk, then, of the courts 'regulating' government might seem a little odd to some readers. However, the term need not be defined too narrowly. Baldwin and Cave (1999: 2) note that it can be used in three different senses, ranging from a specific set of commands, to deliberate state influence, to all forms of social control or influence. Like Collins (1999: 7), I am using 'regulation' as a 'generic term to describe a set of rules intended to govern the behaviour of its subjects'. As Tomkins has recently noted (2003: 18) 'public law regulates the enterprise of government'. By placing the influence of judicial review in regulatory perspective, it focuses our attention on the behaviour-modifying function ascribed to judicial review judgments and permits us to assess the effectiveness of judicial review litigation as an enforcement mechanism. Further, there is a strong tradition in the regulation literature of empirical socio-legal research from which administrative law scholarship has much to gain (Richardson, 2004). The relationships between prescriptive rules, enforcement practices and the modification of behaviour have been richly explored in the regulation literature, and much insight can be gained from this in thinking about the influence of judicial review on government administration. In many ways, these are parallel enterprises.

Regulatory Standards and Regulatory Goals

However, there is perhaps a risk of confusion in analysing the influence of judicial review from a regulatory perspective which should be explored carefully. Many studies in regulation ultimately seek to assess the effectiveness of regulatory enforcement in achieving the goals of the regulatory scheme. For example, one might assess the effectiveness of enforcement practices in relation to health and safety regulation in reducing workplace accidents. Or, one might assess the effectiveness of competition law regulation in achieving a healthy, competitive market. So, one might empirically assess whether and to what extent enforcement practices are effective in securing compliance with regulatory standards but ultimately be interested in whether compliance with regulatory standards is effective in achieving the regulatory goals. In other words, much regulation scholarship is concerned with exploring empirically the relationship between compliance with regulatory standards and the attainment of regulatory goals.[3] Cane (forthcoming) has pointed out recently that this is an aspect of regulation scholarship which has been missing from judicial review impact studies. Most studies of the impact of judicial review on administrative decision-making simply want to know whether and to what extent judicial review is effective in securing compliance with its regulatory standards—that is, the principles of administrative law as applied in judicial review in order to guide decision-makers about how particular decision-making processes should occur. There is a lack of research which then goes on explicitly to assess whether compliance with administrative law 'regulatory standards' (as fixed through judicial review judgments) is effective in achieving the regulatory goal of administrative law.[4] Indeed, as Cane points out, the regulatory goal of administrative law is usually assumed rather than explicitly discussed in such studies, particularly in the UK. Unless, he suggests, the norms of administrative law can be related to some external, underlying goal(s), existing impact studies get perilously close to a tautology to the effect that the purpose of administrative law is to secure compliance with administrative law. This is a powerful claim.

The Regulatory Goal of Administrative Law

Vincent-Jones has noted:

> In many fields the fundamental regulatory purposes and underlying values may be relatively self-evident or uncontentious, as in control of recognised 'harms' involving accidents and ill-health at work, cataclysmic damage to

---

[3] Yeung (2004), however, is critical of a confusion of the two in some studies which talk about 'securing compliance'.

[4] For a related, though perhaps more fundamental, critique of some regulation literature, see Vincent-Jones (2002).

the environment, or high prices caused by producers' inefficiencies and excessive profits and wages. Problems of evaluation are multiplied in other regulatory contexts in which regulatory goals are not so obvious, where the harms are not so clear-cut, or there are choices to be made between conflicting public goods. (2002: 32)

Administrative law, it is suggested, is one of those fields where the identification of regulatory goals is a tricky business. Nevertheless, it should be noted at the outset that this study seeks to contribute to our understanding of judicial review litigation as a regulatory mechanism in pursuit of good administration within government. However, it stops short of attempting to justify this as a regulatory goal for administrative law. Such would be beyond the scope of this enquiry. Suffice it to say that the notion that administrative law embodies principles of good administration is sufficiently prominent within UK administrative law scholarship that the positing of 'good administration' as a regulatory goal for judicial review—even as a theoretical premise—renders this research of at least some value to the field (Baldwin and McCrudden, 1987: 70). More significantly, however, this study also stops short of defining 'good administration' by looking outside the confines of legal doctrine. Instead, its concern is with the effectiveness of judicial review in securing compliance with administrative law's own standards of good administration. But this, it should be noted, avoids Cane's warning about tautologies.

The difficulty with the concept of 'good administration' is that its meaning is particularly amorphous and elusive.[5] Indeed, its meaning is sufficiently contested that it makes the job of relating the regulatory standards of judicial review to the regulatory goal of administrative law especially tricky. In order to be able to consider empirically whether and to what extent compliance with the standards of judicial review contributes to the attainment of the regulatory goal of administrative law, one first has to answer the exclusively normative question of 'what is good administration?'. There is a lack of agreement about the set of principles which are applicable or the considerations which should be taken into account in judging what 'good administration' requires. For example, administrative law doctrine certainly comprises one authoritative system. But alongside administrative law, there are other formal accountability regimes, such as the Ombudsman, or the

---

[5] Almost as elusive and unhelpful as the notion of the will of Parliament (see Allen, 2003).

Charter Mark regime, which also lay claim to being repositories of principles of good administration in the public sector. In addition, academic scholarship may offer normative accounts of good administration or administrative justice (see, for example, Galligan, 1996). Additionally, of course, senses of good administration may be organically generated on the ground by those engaged in administration.

The matter is complicated further by that the fact that 'good administration' as a concept requires application in a real context to take on substance. This presents another challenge for identifying the regulatory goal of administrative law. The normative systems or theories noted above usually offer only a general *approach*—a set of tools— for resolving the problem of what good administration entails on the ground. None of them offer a definitive, recognisable regulatory goal against which judicial review could be assessed in the specific as a regulatory mechanism. Although 'good administration' may be intelligible as a concept, the question still remains of which *conception* of good administration is best in any given context. To answer this, one would have to opt for one or other of the available sets of principles (or develop a new one), apply it in a specific context, then assess whether judicial review had been effective in promoting those requirements of good administration in that particular context.

Two Levels of a 'Regulatory Perspective'

It seems, then, that judicial review can be put into 'regulatory perspective' at two levels. First, one might consider the extent to which judicial review is effective in securing compliance with administrative law as developed by the court in relation to a specific context. Secondly, one might consider the extent to which compliance with administrative law is effective in fulfilling the regulatory goal of 'good administration'. The first question is empirical (though also requires legal analysis). The second requires normative theorising before proceeding to empirical analysis. Together they constitute a comprehensive enquiry. There is undoubtedly room for work within administrative law scholarship which makes the link between the two levels, but the aims of this book are more modest. My interest is in the court's ability to fashion government administration in its own image(s) of administrative justice as developed and applied in a piecemeal fashion to particular issues in government decision-making. Admittedly, this goes only part-way to putting judicial review's influence in regulatory perspective. But careful empirical groundwork is an essential and discrete stage of the enterprise. And it avoids the risk of tautology because the study does not claim that the purpose of administrative law it to achieve compliance with administrative law. Rather it is premised on the assertion that the purpose of administrative law is (in part at least) to promote good administration within government. The limit of the study is that it does not seek to engage in the normative work necessary to complete the comprehensive enquiry. But given the size of such a normative enquiry, the fact that for administrative law it constitutes a discrete stage in the regulatory approach, and the constitutional significance of the courts when expounding its visions of good administration, I hope this can be forgiven.

The Various Functions of Judicial Review

At this point we can return to the previous discussion about the various functions of judicial review. It was noted above that, although one may ascribe various functions to judicial review, this study is focusing solely on its capacity to secure compliance with the regulatory standards of administrative law. This raises a question, however, which should be explored briefly at this point: how does the existence of additional functions of judicial review affect the process of placing judicial review in regulatory perspective? The answer is that it matters a great deal if these additional functions constitute or relate to the regulatory goal of administrative law. However, once again, it is important to stress here the focus of this project. This project does not attempt to engage in the difficult work of discussing the regulatory goal of administrative law. Rather, it simply asserts that the promotion of good administration is *one* regulatory goal, and it provides an empirical analysis which will help us think about judicial review's regulatory effectiveness in securing compliance with the courts' own standards of good administration. It is not suggested that this is the end point of either socio-legal administrative law scholarship, or even the more specific task of thinking about judicial review's influence in regulatory perspective. There is a whole additional layer of enquiry where the regulatory goal(s) of administrative law are explored in depth, and its/their relationship to compliance with the courts' standards of good administration is examined in fullness. This kind of enquiry might shed surprising light on the importance of complying with the courts' mandates about good administration to the overall purpose(s) of administrative law. But that is another project and another book. The contribution of this study is clearly limited, though I would argue still important, interesting and useful.

The Heuristic Device

A final word should be offered about the central heuristic device around which this book is structured. In the remainder of this book I set out a series of hypotheses about the conditions which will enhance judicial review's effectiveness in securing compliance with administrative law. The device, as we can see, is fairly simple, and its purpose is fairly modest. It is intended to help us think about the conditions which make a difference to the ability of judicial review to control government behaviour. The basic idea is straightforward: the more these conditions are in existence, the greater will be the influence of judicial review. The less they are present, the weaker judicial review's influence will be.

However, despite the simplicity of the device, a few tricky questions might be asked about it which should be explored at the outset—particularly its relationship to the goal of putting the influence of judicial review in regulatory perspective.

What is the Level of Optimal Compliance?

One question which may be asked concerns the image of optimal compliance inherent in the heuristic device. By talking in terms of effectiveness in securing compliance, does a vision of optimal compliance lurk somewhere beneath the surface? How 'effective' do we expect judicial review to be in modifying behaviour? There may be a temptation to imagine that I am positing a picture of 'perfect compliance' where the guidance issued by the courts through judicial review litigation about how to make certain decisions is followed by all relevant administrative decision-makers all the time (at least until the court changes its mind). This should strike most (perhaps all) readers as a ludicrous notion of judicial review's potential influence. It is. We should be careful not to exaggerate the potential influence of the courts in society (Feeley, 1992). That is not my aim. Instead, by setting out the conditions which will enhance judicial review's effectiveness in securing compliance with administrative law, we should be able to see the limits of judicial review's influence and have the tools to understand *why* this is so. The hypotheses are not supposed to represent reality, nor even the possibility of reality.

Is Perfect Compliance the Regulatory Goal of Judicial Review?

More significantly, perhaps, there may be a temptation to take from the heuristic device the notion that an idea of 'perfect compliance' is the target to which judicial review should strive in terms of 'effectiveness'. This may strike some (perhaps many) as a fanciful target to attach to judicial review as an enforcement mechanism. It is important to note at the outset that it is not intended to have this role. The heuristic device, which should help us think empirically about judicial review's influence on government administration, is in no way a veiled normative argument about the level of behavioural modification which we *should* expect of decision-makers in the wake of judicial review. This question, which is part and parcel of the regulatory goal discussion, is simply left unexplored. What this heuristic device is intended to do is to help us think about what factors *inhibit* the ability of judicial review to secure compliance with its own standards of good administrative behaviour; or, conversely, to think about what conditions will *enhance* the positive impact of judicial review on the relevant administrative world. The heuristic device of hypothesising about the conditions for maximising compliance with administrative law, it should be stressed, is no more than a device. Its aim is to help us think (and conduct research) about the effectiveness of judicial review in influencing administrative behaviour towards the terms of judicial guidance about what good administration entails on the ground. It is hoped that readers find it helpful, but it should be noted it is just one of a number of devices that might have been used. One might easily have turned it on its head and started from the conditions under which judicial review judgments will have no impact at all.

Weight of Individual Conditions

A further important point about the heuristic device must be made. What it cannot do is weight the various conditions described in the analysis in terms of their particular significance to the effectiveness of judicial review as a modifier of administrative behaviour. In other words, we cannot conclude on the basis of this study that one condition is more crucial to judicial review's effectiveness than another (which may be more important than a third, and so on). The value of the heuristic device set out in this book is, unfortunately, less precise, and the aims of the study more modest. What is offered is a set of empirically grounded propositions about the factors which mediate the influence of judicial review on administrative behaviour. The benefit of this contribution, however, is that it permits us to speculate in the round that the more the conditions are present in social reality, the greater will be the influence of judicial review. Further, it provides a series of hypotheses which can be used to develop research which aims to begin the process of weighting the factors and conditions relative to each other—ie, to test the significance of particular factors or conditions to the effectiveness of judicial review in securing compliance with its standards of good administration. In other words, it is hoped that the analysis of this book will lay a foundation for future research which may considerably enhance our understanding of the influence of judicial review on administrative decision-making.

Questions of Degree

A final point follows on from the above. It is important to recognise the conditions discussed throughout this book can be present in varying degrees. Their existence is not an 'either/or' matter. Administrative lawyers are fond of talking about 'questions of fact and degree'. This notion parallels the framing of these conditions. And the heuristic device operates around this basic idea. The conditions for enhancing compliance can be present to a greater or lesser degree. The more they are present, the more effective judicial review will be in securing compliance with administrative law. The less they are present, the less effective it will be.

We will have cause to return to this particular discussion in the concluding chapter where I will offer some further reflections and refinements about the analytical framework constructed throughout the book. However, having explored the heuristic device in sufficient depth to give one a basic grasp of the enterprise, we may now move on to consider some details about the research methods employed—not just the precise research techniques used, but the general approach adopted to investigating the influence of judicial review on administration. These are offered to inform the reader of the some of the theoretical premises which underpinned the research and to allow him/her to assess the book's conclusions in light of the data obtained and their method of collection.

Research Approach

The basic approach of this study was to investigate the influence of judicial review on routine administrative decision-making by examining the decision-making practices of government agencies which had been the subject of judicial review litigation. The aim was to gain an understanding of how decisions are made on the ground, to appreciate the influences on the uses of discretion, and the conditions which inform the decision-making process. This was done in order to be able to explore how (if at all) experiences of judicial review interacted with other influences in the administrative arena. As we will discover in the chapters which follow, the process of routine administrative decision-making is not a straightforward business, but is rather subject to a number of pressures. To understand the complexity of routine government behaviour, we should try as researchers to get as close to it as we can. The closer we get, the easier it is to unpack the range of influences on government decision-making and see the subtleties of discretion at work.

By gaining an understanding of how administrative decisions were made, and by observing the influences and factors which routinely informed the decision-making process *but were in conflict* with the requirements of administrative law as expressed through judicial review, I have been able to tease out the barriers to judicial review's influence. In essence, this book constitutes an empirical study of non-compliance. An appreciation of the barriers to judicial review's positive influence in the three housing authorities which took part in the research allows us to speculate more generally about the factors which mediate the effectiveness of judicial review as a modifier of ongoing administrative behaviour. The heuristic device which is used throughout this book is also intended as an analytical framework which may be useful for future research. It is hoped that many of the empirical details presented in the chapters which follow will prove interesting and enlightening for readers. However, their basic purpose is to illustrate and support the central hypotheses which constitute the analytical framework for thinking about judicial review's capacity to fashion administrative decision-making towards its own image(s) of good administration. The analysis of this book, as already noted above, is not intended as a final word on judicial review's influence, but is rather meant to offer a starting point—an empirically grounded foundation for taking the research agenda forward.

Research Techniques

Fieldwork took place in three sites between October 1996 and September 1998. Three months' participant observation was conducted in each site. Post-observation interviews were also conducted in order to test further the themes which had emerged from the participant observation work. Excerpts from these interviews are used illustratively throughout the text in presenting the data. Participant observation was chosen as a principal research technique because it offered the greatest chance of obtaining naturalistic data about the administrative process. The benefit of participant observation is that it promises the best opportunity for the researcher to *experience* the social world under study. As Emerson, Fretz and Straw (1995: 2) have noted,

> the field researcher must be able to take up positions in the midst of key sites and scenes of other's lives in order to observe and understand them. But getting close has another, far more significant component: the ethnographer seeks a deeper *immersion* in others' worlds in order to grasp what they experience as meaningful and important. With immersion, the field researcher sees from the inside how people lead their lives, how they carry out their daily rounds of activities, what they find meaningful, and how they do so. In this way immersion gives the fieldworker access to the fluidity of others' lives and enhances his sensitivity to interaction and process.

Implicit to this approach is a starting point which holds that meanings are imposed upon the social world by individuals (Schutz, 1967). Social reality is constructed by each of us through interpretive processes. These processes of interpretation take place within what might be termed 'interpretive communities' (Fish, 1989). Shared meanings and understandings emerge and evolve within interpretive communities. These communities are infinite and various and are neither closed nor mutually exclusive. As Fish remarks of himself, 'I am, among other things, white, male, a teacher, a literary critic, a student of interpretation, a member of a law faculty, a husband (twice), a citizen . . .' (1989:30).

The starting point, therefore, is at the level of the individual, in the sense that we encounter the world pre-interpretively as individuals (Schutz, 1967). However, a picture of interpretive communities illustrates how the meaning comes about in the social world. Although our absolute starting point may be individualistic, we learn to understand our worlds in community. In relation to organisational decision-making, or more particularly as we shall see in due course, in relation to decision-making within a single team of bureaucrats, individuals become initiated into the interpretive schema of the team. As new officers (and, indeed, as participant-observers) 'learn the job', so they come to learn what meanings are attached to the phenomena that make up the subject and fabric of the administrative process. As regards organisational matters, therefore, the interpretive mandate comes substantially from the organisation itself. Of course, decision-making within an organisation is subject to influences from outside it. Organisations work according to legal and policy mandates, and operate within broader social, political and economic contexts which feed into both the organisational mandate(s) and also the interpretive work of individuals. An appreciation of the decision-making environment, as we will see further in chapter 5, is important to a full understanding of the decision-making process. Nevertheless, the organisation is a strong interpretive filter by which workers come to understand the business of the organisation (Cicourel, 1968; Waegel, 1981; Emerson and Paley, 1992) and so attention to the shared meanings and organisational interpretive schema, then, becomes central to our understanding of decision-making.

Choice of Research Subjects

The government agencies which took part in the study were local government homeless persons units (HPUs). As we will see in greater detail below, homelessness law offers positive housing rights for certain groups of people in housing need. The task of implementing homelessness law—deciding who qualifies under the legal criteria, and performing the consequent duties—has been delegated by Parliament to local authorities. At the time of initial fieldwork, aggrieved applicants' only form of legal redress was to apply for judicial review of the local authority's decision.[6] Homelessness decision-making, resultantly, was the subject of a very high volume of judicial review applications and formed one of the 'core areas' of the High Court's overall judicial review workload (Bridges, Meszaros and Sunkin, 1996). The position in Scotland was similar (Mullen et al, 1996), though not so in Northern Ireland, perhaps due to the internal review and appeals mechanisms within the Northern Ireland Housing Executive (Hadfield & Weaver, 1995).

The particular local authorities with whom research was conducted were selected according to their level of exposure to judicial review litigation. In comparison to their peers, they had considerable experience of defending judicial review actions. Indeed, they were among the most heavily litigated homeless persons units in England and Wales.[7] Further, in relation to each authority, the content of the judicial review litigation was broad, covering a wide range of the grounds of review concerning the decision-making process. The decision to conduct research with heavily litigated agencies was part of the aim of testing the ability of judicial review to positively influence the administrative process. For (hypothetically at least) it would be in these extreme cases, if anywhere, that judicial review would have played an 'hortatory role' (Loveland, 1995: 280). Greater confidence can be had about the barriers to judicial review's influence by observing them in relation to agencies which had experienced considerable exposure to the court's scrutiny, as opposed to those which had experienced little or none.

It should be noted, however, that in determining which housing authorities were 'heavily litigated', attention was given only to judicial review applications which had reached the stage of court hearings—particularly the stage of the court delivering its judgment. This is not to suggest that it is not important to study settlement practices in relation to judicial review litigation (Fisher and Schmidt, 2001). A number of studies have demonstrated the significance of settlement practices to understanding the impact of judicial review (see, for example, Dotan, 1999; Bridges et al, 2000). However, the choice to conduct research

[6] Since then a right of internal administrative review of adverse decisions has been granted to aggrieved applicants under the Housing Act 1996. The failure to take up rights of internal review, and the processes of applying for and determining internal review has been the subject of a recent empirical study by Cowan and Halliday (2003).

[7] All three subject authorities fell within the ten most litigated homeless persons units in England and Wales according to a combined search of the *Lexis* database, *Current Law* and the law reports. Muirfield and Timbergreens fell within the top three.

with housing authorities which had been 'heavily litigated' (in the sense in which I am using this phrase) was based on the desire to work with administrators whose decisions had been subject to full review and comment by judges. Such experience, it is suggested, symbolises the fullest immersion of the administrative decision-making process into the legal world.

It is perhaps appropriate at this stage to offer some details about the local authorities which took part in the study and to give a brief sketch of their character. They have been called Timbergreens, Muirfield and Eastbank.[8] Each of them is situated in a large urban area within England.

Timbergreens

Levels of applications to Timbergreens' HPU for help with housing were high. Over two thousand households would make applications for assistance as homeless people in a given year. Many others approached the HPU for help but were not recorded for statistical purposes. The HPU comprised four sub-sections—Casework, Rehousing, Finance and Temporary Accommodation. Fieldwork was spent exclusively with the casework team, the job of which was to make decisions as to what duties were owed to homeless applicants under homelessness law. The casework team had one manager, three team leaders, thirteen caseworkers, and two administrative staff. The caseworkers were divided into three teams, each with their own team leader. The team leaders were responsible for making decisions on the cases passed to them by their team. The manager oversaw all the case-work in this section, although not being directly involved in it, and managed the personnel within it. There were two grades of casework-ers. These grades reflected different salaries and, accordingly, different responsibilities within the overall case work. Higher grade casework-ers were allocated what were considered to be the most difficult cases. Lower grade caseworkers were allocated less difficult cases. The case-work team was marked by a particular longevity of service from the staff. At the time of fieldwork, the least amount of continuous years worked by an officer in the team was four years. The manager had worked in the team for twelve years. The team leaders had worked in the HPU for ten, fifteen and twenty years respectively.

---

[8] After my childhood schools.

The first homelessness judicial review case involving Timbergreens which went to judgment occurred in the late 1980s. Timbergreens had not kept any systematic record of judicial review litigation. However, the minimum number of substantive judicial review hearings in which they had been involved by the time of fieldwork was 22 with a further minimum of 11 challenges reaching the stage of an application for leave being heard by the court.[9] This figure does not include judicial reviews which comprised a challenge to the suitability of the permanent accommodation offered to successful homeless applicants. Such decisions about suitability of permanent housing were made by the Rehousing Team within the HPU and as such were not the focus of fieldwork. Timbergreens' HPU as a whole had also been involved in other judicial review litigation concerning its functions. These cases have also been excluded from the above figure.

Timbergreens may be characterised as a team of workers who were, generally speaking, quite conscientious about acting lawfully. There was an evident professional concern to discern what the law required of them (or enabled them to do), to maintain legal knowledge within the team and to meet the demands of what it understood to be lawful decision-making. Legal knowledge and skills were accorded professional respect. The team as a whole prided itself on being 'good' at law and maintained a programme to keep its officers up to date with legal developments. It also formally consulted with legal officers concerning certain types of decision. A number of the officers displayed quite sophisticated knowledge about the intricacies of homelessness law. However, as we shall see in due course, competing priorities within the decision-making environment regularly trumped their commitment to legality, and their legal knowledge was not always used to comply with the spirit of administrative law. Like each of the case study local authorities, Timbergreens suffered from a temporary accommodation deficit and some of its casework was fashioned around trying to manage the demand for temporary bed and breakfast accommodation. The volume of homelessness applications placed significant stress on individual officers and the routine business of decision-making was heavily influenced by the need to process applications quickly—moving cases from one's own desk on to that of another. The never-ending tide of

[9] The figures for all three research subjects are based on an examination of all judicial review applications involving those local authorities recorded on the *Lexis* database, reported in the law reports—*Housing Law Reports, All England Law Reports and Weekly Law Reports*, and recorded in *Current Law*.

new applications prioritised the efficient handling of cases and placed limits on the quality of casework that could be undertaken. Timbergreens also received a significant number of applications from ethnic minority applicants, many from southern Asia, and there was considerable evidence of organisational suspicion and systemic discrimination (discussed more fully in Halliday, 2000b).

Muirfield

Homelessness applications to Muirfield were also very high and the HPU was a busy organisation. Almost four thousand new applications were made during the year in which fieldwork took place. Muirfield's HPU comprised seven sub-sections: the administration section, the housing register team, the rehousing section, the temporary accommodation section, a private sector housing rights team, the assessments and advice section, and the casework team. Fieldwork was spent mostly with the casework team, though an initial period was spent observing the assessments and advice section. This section was responsible for conducting initial assessments in relation to all homelessness applications. Assessments and advice officers interviewed all homeless applicants and determined whether referral to the casework was required. Such referrals would be made if the assessments officer believed the applicant to be both homeless and in priority need.

The casework team was responsible for determining homeless applications which were referred to it by the assessments and advice team. It investigated homeless applications and decided what legal duties, if any, were owed to applicants. The casework section was made up of two teams, each with six caseworkers and one team leader. Its work was overseen by a manager. In general, workers within the casework team had worked there for considerable time, though less so when compared with Timbergreens. The manager had worked in the HPU for eight years. The team leaders had worked there for six and ten years respectively.

Muirfield's experiences of judicial reviews began in the early 1980s, but increased considerably during the 1990s. Neither the casework team nor the legal department kept any systematic record of its judicial review litigation. However, it can be estimated that up until the end of fieldwork, Muirfield's casework team had defended forty-two judicial reviews, of which four had stopped at the application for leave stage.

In comparison with Timbergreens, Muirfield was notably compla-
cent about the demands of law. As an organisation, Muirfield's HPU
may be characterised as treating law as an environmental nuisance (see
Cooper, 1995). Politically, Muirfield displayed a strong antipathy
towards homeless applicants. Practically, this translated into a highly
restrictive approach to the provision of assistance. Such an approach
sat comfortably with an ethos created by the demands of managing a
heavy and constant caseload. Like Timbergreens, Muirfield suffered
from a significant shortage of adequate temporary accommodation.
Together these environmental pressures produced a climate where a
stress was placed on deterring applications and efficiently resolving
those that were successfully made. The stress on efficiency, as we shall
see in greater detail in due course, was formalised through a system of
performance related pay. Judicial reviews were viewed as an unwelcome obstacle to the goals of efficiency and minimal assistance,
though not one which particularly troubled the organisation. Muirfield
had deep pockets and robustly defended litigation as a matter of course
and as part of its minimalist policy towards the homeless. This is not to
say, however, that all officers shared Muirfield's politics or attitudes
towards homelessness assistance. Instead, the HPU was a site of internal struggle where juniors officers would engage in subversive decision-
making in the attempt to impose a covert welfarist discourse on the
administrative process, though ultimately without success.

Eastbank

Eastbank's HPU was similarly a busy organisation. During the year in
which fieldwork took place, it received over two thousand homelessness applications. Like Timbergreens, additional persons approached
it for help with housing but were not registered as having formally
made an application, usually because their application was dealt with
verbally and summarily. Eastbank estimated that these numbered over
500 people annually.

The HPU was headed up by a senior manager and was made up of
six teams—the casework team, the temporary accommodation team,
the resettlement team, the rehousing team, the finance and systems
team and the customer services team. The casework team was responsible for making decisions on housing applications from homeless
persons, and it was this team with which fieldwork was conducted. It
comprised three teams of caseworkers, each with its own team leader.

There were four caseworkers in each team. The operations of case-work were supervised by a manager. Eastbank also enjoyed the services of unemployed persons seeking work experience. During fieldwork there were two people gaining such experience on a part-time basis. Like Timbergreens, there was a marked longevity of service within Eastbank's casework team. Many, though not all, of the officers had worked in the team for a very long time. The manager had worked in casework for fourteen years. Two of the team leaders had worked there for over nine years, and the third had worked there for five years.

In terms of judicial review litigation, Eastbank was the least experi-enced of the three local authorities which took part in the study. Nevertheless, its experience was still substantial. It was also relatively recent compared with that of Timbergreens and Muirfield. Its first experience of defending judicial review proceedings concerning homelessness decision-making was in the early 1990s. At this time it experienced a notable increase in judicial review litigation which, although tailing off quite quickly, remained constant up until the period of fieldwork. No systematic record was kept by Eastbank con-cerning the volume of judicial review applications it had defended. However, the minimum number of judicial reviews which Eastbank had defended in court by the time of fieldwork was nineteen. Five of these involved decision-making of the resettlement (re-housing) team. If these are discounted, the figure for judicial review litigation for case-work team decision-making is fourteen, three of which ceased at application for leave stage.

Eastbank may be characterised as an organisation in a prolonged state of crisis. As we shall see in greater detail in chapter 5, the pressure of a limited stock of available bed and breakfast establishments combined with a large number of applications, meant that much of Eastbank's casework was driven by the attempt to avoid the placement of applicants in temporary accommodation. Although this was an evident pressure in each of the case studies, it was particularly acute in Eastbank by virtue of the fact that it was trying to address a 10 per cent overspend on its temporary accommodation budget at the time of field-work. The need to make financial savings was an overriding concern which fed directly into compromised and unlawful casework practices. Individual officers displayed, generally speaking, less sophistication in legal matters when compared with officers of Muirfield and Timbergreens. This was in part a product of the containment of legal knowledge within the HPU, a matter discussed further in chapter 2.

Any desire to disseminate legal knowledge gained from litigation or to engage in the training of officers was usually overwhelmed by the more immediate demands of managing the constant flow of cases in a way which minimised expenditure. This is not to say, however, that Eastbank did not care about the treatment of individuals as the subjects of the administrative process. This was indeed an organisational concern. However, the plight of the homeless person was framed more in terms of customer satisfaction than in terms of legality. A great deal of stress was placed within Eastbank on constructing the image of the HPU as an organisation committed to customer care. Eastbank as a whole had taken on the values of New Public Management and was keen to instil some market values into its service delivery. The housing department had the status of an autonomous 'business unit' within Eastbank and contracted its services to the council. A number of organisational initiatives were undertaken to be able to demonstrate evidence of customer care and business efficiency. For example, the HPU had gained ISO9000 accreditation, a British Standards in Industry quality assurance award. Applicants were re-titled 'customers' and receptionists were employed as 'customer service officers'. A stress was placed on responding to customer queries timeously and resolving applications quickly.

The sketches above about the character of the respective case study local authorities are intended to give readers a rough sense of the organisations which were studied before we embark on the central analysis of the book. Further details about the operations of the Timbergreens, Muirfield and Eastbank will emerge in the chapters which follow as the data from fieldwork is used to illustrate and support the analytical framework about the conditions which mediate judicial review's influence on government administration. Before this can happen, however, we must also consider the nature of homelessness law, and it is to this matter that we now turn.

AN OVERVIEW OF HOMELESSNESS LAW

Much has been written about the social and political history of homelessness law, not least as part of recent empirical studies of its administration in local government (Loveland, 1995; Cowan, 1997; Cowan and Halliday, 2003). Those who are interested in the history of this interesting and, in international terms, fairly unique feature of the UK's welfare state provision, are referred to those books and the studies cited therein. The absence of a discussion of this literature here is quite deliberate. My study of administrative decision-making in the complex social and political field of homelessness law and social welfare policy has been distilled to produce an analytical framework which will be useful for thinking about the capacity of judicial review to secure compliance with administrative law generally—considerably beyond the confines of this small, though fascinating, corner of public law. The lack of contextual detail at this level may prove slightly frustrating for some readers, though it is necessary to help us focus analytically, and therefore generally, on the relationship between judicial review and bureaucratic behaviour.

There are additionally a number of scholarly doctrinal analyses of homelessness law (Arden and Hunter, 2002; Robson and Poustie, 1996), and readers with an interest in gaining a close knowledge of the legal provisions and their interpretation in the courts are referred to these works. Nevertheless, it is appropriate at this stage to offer a brief overview of the structure and basic content of homelessness law so that the reader may gain a sufficient grasp of the legal scheme being administered by the research subjects. At the beginning of fieldwork, the law was governed by the Housing Act 1985.

The Homeless Persons' Obstacle Race

Homelessness law has been likened to an obstacle race which the homelessness applicant is required to negotiate in order to win the right to housing (Robson and Watchman, 1981). This remains a helpful metaphor for understanding the basic structure of the law. There were three primary obstacles—homelessness, priority need and intentionality. If these obstacles were successfully negotiated (ie, the applicant was homeless, had a priority need, and was not intentionally homeless) then the local authority had a duty to ensure that accommodation became available to the housing applicant. Under certain circumstances the housing authority had the discretion to refer this duty to another housing authority.

Homelessness

Homelessness was defined on three levels, the first of which related to rooflessness—where the applicant simply had no accommodation. The second level related to applicants who had accommodation but insufficient legal status as an occupier to be regarded as not homeless. The third level concerned applicants who had accommodation and sufficient legal status as occupiers, but where there was some difficulty with occupying it. Accommodation would be unacceptable in this way where, for example, occupation would probably have lead to violence, or where it would not have been reasonable for the applicant to continue to occupy the accommodation.

Priority Need

Housing rights, however, were not afforded to all homeless people. Instead the legislation set out groups of people who had a 'priority need' and only those who fell within one of the groups would successfully negotiate this second hurdle. Those who had a priority need were, for example, people with dependant children, or those who were vulnerable due to old age, mental illness, physical disability or other special reason.

Intentionality

The third obstacle related to 'intentional homelessness'. Applicants were treated as having become homeless intentionally if they had deliberately done (or had failed to do) something which resulted in them ceasing to occupy accommodation which it would have been reasonable to continue occupying. If applicants were determined to be intentionally homeless, they were disqualified from housing.

Local Connection

The issue of 'local connection' came into play if the applicant had successfully negotiated the first three obstacles, thus gaining a right to permanent accommodation. A local authority could only transfer the housing obligation if the applicant did not have a local connection with it, and did have a local connection with another local authority in Great Britain, and would not run the risk of domestic violence in that local authority area. Local connection was determined by the following factors: the applicant was, or had been in the past, normally resident in the area; the applicant was employed in the area; the applicant had family associations in the area; or, there were special circumstances which gave rise to a local connection.

Legislative Changes During Fieldwork

During the course of fieldwork, homelessness law was amended in England and Wales. During fieldwork with Timbergreens, the legislation was contained in Part III of the Housing Act 1985. During fieldwork with Muirfield and Eastbank, homelessness law was governed by Part VII of the Housing Act 1996. This change, however, is not too important for the purposes of this research. The basic structure of the rules about entitlement to housing remained largely the same.[10] The most significant changes to the law related to the housing duties of local authorities where homeless applicants were successful in completing the 'obstacle race'.[11] The new legislation also introduced a right to an internal review of local authority decisions[12] and a right of appeal on a point of law to the county court.[13]

A BRIEF OVERVIEW OF THE BOOK

Having described the research methods used in this study and given a very basic introduction to the main provisions of homelessness law at the time of fieldwork, it remains in this chapter to offer an overview of the rest of the book. As indicated at the outset, the book builds an analytical framework for thinking about the extent to which judicial review can positively influence the administrative processes of government agencies. The chapters which follow explore in turn the list of

---

[10] Some changes, however, were made to the rules about initial entitlement. The definition of homelessness was amended to exclude from assistance those who had accommodation anywhere in the world (Housing Act 1996, s 175(1)). Under the 1985 Act the geographical boundary stopped at Great Britain. The definition of intentional homelessness was also extended to specifically include the situations where, first, an applicant gives up accommodation specifically to take advantage of the homelessness legislation (s 191(3)), and secondly, where an applicant fails to take up accommodation in the private sector having been provided with sufficient advice and assistance to enable her to do so (s 191(4)).

[11] In contrast to the long-term housing duty under the Housing Act 1985, under the Housing Act 1996 local authorities are only required to provide a minimum of two years' accommodation to successful homeless applicants (s 193). This accommodation duty is then reviewed biannually (s 194).

[12] Housing Act 1996, s 202.

[13] Ibid, s 204.

hypotheses about the conditions which will enhance the effectiveness of judicial review in securing compliance with administrative law. There is one final task to be completed, however, before the list of hypotheses can be set out. First, the administrative realm—the social world of government administration—must be sub-divided into three constituent elements: (1) the decision-makers; (2) the environment in which decisions are made; and (3) the law. The hypotheses about the conditions for maximising compliance will be grouped in relation to individual elements, and the book as a whole is divided into sections reflecting these elements.

Part 2: The Decision-Makers

Part two of the book considers the decision-makers within government agencies. There are three hypotheses to explore here. First, chapter 2 argues that compliance with administrative law will be enhanced where decision-makers receive the message about administrative justice or good administration being communicated by the court. However, it goes on to demonstrate the considerable barriers which stand in the way of a full reception of legal knowledge into administrative agencies. The complexity of administrative organisations adds a new complexion to the requirement of legal knowledge. Administrative 'decisions' are often produced from the discretion of multiple actors at different levels of an organisation. This means that legal knowledge must not only be received by an agency, it must also be dispersed *within* the agency. The complexity of organisations, however, can incline towards the containment of legal knowledge within particulars groups of personnel. The role of legal advisors is also important to the extent of legal knowledge within government.

Secondly, chapter 3 argues that the more conscientious decision-makers are about applying their legal knowledge to their routine tasks, the more effective will judicial review be in securing compliance with administrative law. Simply knowing what the law requires of you as a decision-maker is not enough. The case study data, however, similarly demonstrates that there is much in the business of administrative decision-making which prevails against the flourishing of legal conscientiousness. The chapter explores the salience of professional intuition and cultures of suspicion as forms of internal normative ordering which weaken the normative influence of law. It also shows how legal knowledge may be used to creatively comply with administrative law and how the process of judicial review may, paradoxically, operate to reduce a faith in law to produce the right decision-outcome.

Thirdly, chapter 4 sets out the hypothesis that compliance will be enhanced by an increasing level of legal competence on the part of the decision-makers. By 'legal competence', I refer to an ability to extract general legal principles from particular judicial review judgments, then re-apply them to other similar decision-making processes within decision-makers' remit. This chapter draws our attention to the question of the interpretation of law by administrative organisations, noting that there can be an interpretive gap between the courts and the administration and that the relational distance between the two militates against the development of an interpretive synergy. The chapter also argues that the bureaucratic mode of operation, by its very nature, inhibits legal competence. Bureaucracies operate by way of rules and formal rationality. By conscientiously and consistently following a precise ruling from a judicial review decision in future relevant cases, the government bureaucracy may be faithful to the letter of administrative law, but will often miss its spirit. The chapter additionally explores the bounded application of legal knowledge by government agencies and observes the strange paradox that an increased exposure to judicial review can contribute to a reduction in the extent to which government agencies self-regulate their compliance with administrative law.

Part 3: The Decision-Making Environment

Chapter 5 considers the decision-making environment, and uses the empirical data from the study to illustrate the various and competing pressures that can co-exist within the administrative arena. It sets out the hypothesis that judicial review's ability to secure compliance with administrative law will be enhanced where the competition between law and other normative systems is reduced, or where law's strength in the environment is increased. Assessing what conditions the strength of law is made difficult by the fact that the different normative systems within the environment are constantly being internalised by decision-makers to different extents and at different times. The competition between law and other normative forces is repeatedly played out across many sites within the decision-making process, producing quite a complicated and fragmented picture of the range of administrative values and their relative importance. Nevertheless, drawing on the regulatory enforcement literature, the chapter suggests three conditioning factors: first, the extent to which judicial review operates as a sanction; secondly, the role of negotiation and persuasion in enforcement; and thirdly, the flexibility of law in alternating between sanctioning and persuading enforcement strategies.

Part 4: The Law

The fourth part of the book considers the final element of the administrative realm—the law. It argues that the ability of judicial review to secure compliance with the legal requirements of good administration will be enhanced where the courts project clear and consistent messages about administrative justice in relation to particular decision-making tasks. Chapter 6 begins this discussion by making the simple observation that administrative justice is a contested concept, and illustrates this by reference to some pertinent socio-legal administrative justice scholarship, focusing in particular on the work of Jerry Mashaw in the US and Mike Adler in the UK. Chapters 7 and 8 argue that, just as in the socio-legal scholarship, administrative justice is a similarly contested concept within administrative law doctrine. This magnifies the extent to which the courts may be inconsistent and unclear in spelling out the requirements of administrative justice for different kinds of decision-makers. Chapters 7 and 8 engage in a doctrinal analysis to demonstrate that administrative law is riven by competing priorities and is essentially schizophrenic in character. These chapters describe two parallel competitions which go to the heart of administrative law, and are sufficiently central to its enterprise that it renders the meaning of administrative law contingent for government agencies. Chapter 7 describes the competition between judicial control and agency autonomy, and Chapter 8 describes the competition between individual and agency interests. These competitions, which are played out in the doctrine in relation to various fields of administrative decision-making, produce competing images of administrative justice, some of which are related to the models described in the socio-legal literature. In particular, Chapter 8 suggests that the moral judgment model and the bureaucratic rationality model found in Mashaw's work are reflected in the competition within legal doctrine between individual and agency interests and that, accordingly, Adler is mistaken in describing only the moral judgment model as the 'legality' model.

Part 5: Conclusion

Chapter 9 draws the study to a close and refocuses in the round on the book's aim of developing a framework for analysing the court's ability to fashion government administration in its own image(s) of administrative justice (as developed and applied in a piecemeal fashion to particular issues in government decision-making). It summarises the analytical framework developed throughout the book and considers its potential for application in other fields of government activity. The chapter argues that the framework may be applied beyond the confines of the case study of homelessness law which many may consider to be a peculiar and unrepresentative corner of British public law. In doing so, however, it observes that, in terms of securing compliance with administrative law, there is some level of equilibrium between legal conscientiousness and the extent to which judicial review operates as a sanction which will vary according to context. The chapter concludes with a note on the potential direction of future research concerned with the regulation of government decision-making.

Part 2: The Decision-Makers

2

The Reception of Legal Knowledge into Government Agencies

IN THE PREVIOUS chapter, we set out the aims and structure of the book and noted that it comprises a series of hypotheses about the conditions which will maximise the extent to which judicial review will secure compliance with administrative law. We further noted that these hypotheses are grouped within the three elements which make up the administrative realm—the social world of government administration. This part of the book explores the first element of the administrative realm: that of the decision-makers. In relation to administrative decision-makers, the first hypothesis is that the more the decision-makers receive the legal knowledge from judicial review about what administrative law requires of them, the greater will be judicial review's capacity to secure compliance with administrative law. This hypothesis is the subject of this chapter.

The issue of legal knowledge has been highlighted in a number of studies concerned with the impact of judicial review (Obadina, 1988; Kerry, 1986; Sunkin and Le Sueur, 1991; Creyke and McMillan, 2002). Similarly in relation to the study of regulation, the question of knowledge of regulatory standards is posed as a fundamental concern. Kagan and Scholz (1984) and Baldwin (1995), for example, draw our attention to the 'incompetent' or 'ill-informed' organisation whereby regulators must take on an educative role in order to increase their effectiveness. Parker (1999b) also, in the context of the regulation of sexual harassment within companies, argues that some kind of information dissemination system is essential to securing compliance. A similar point is made by Sossin (2004) in relation to the impact of judicial review on administrative agencies, though he frames his enquiry in terms of 'soft law'. He presents a case study of the impact of judicial review in Canada by way of examining administrative guidelines or protocols developed by administrative agencies in the aftermath of judicial review litigation. Sossin notes that soft law provides a significant window into the relationship between judicial and administrative decision-making and into how judicial and bureaucratic priorities are articulated within government agencies. Soft law, then, is a significant area of enquiry for our understanding of government behaviour. As Hawkins (2002) has observed, the development and transmission of policy within bureaucracies is an important subject which has been relatively neglected in socio-legal studies.

According to Sossin, soft law can take many forms. Indeed, he adopts a particularly wide definition. However, for the purposes of the administration of homelessness law in England and Wales, which formed the basis of this study, we can point to two main forms of soft law: (1) government codes of guidance to local authorities about how to administer homelessness law; and (2) local authorities' internally generated guidance about the legal requirements of homelessness administration.

The government issued an official code of guidance to local authorities (Department of the Environment, 1991) which was intended to provide a detailed account of the legal duties owed to homeless applicants, both in terms of duties of good administration and substantive housing duties, in addition to offering advice about good practice. This is an example of formal soft law. However, administrative organisations themselves may produce internal and informal guidance about how to carry out their functions in a lawful fashion. We will have cause to consider in greater depth the significance of informal soft law to our understanding of how legal mandates are re-interpreted into bureaucratic rationalities. Data will be presented in chapter 4 about the development of informal soft law instruments as a reaction to judicial review and the importance of legal competence to full compliance with administrative law. First, however, in this chapter we consider more practical issues which affect the extent to which legal knowledge is received into administrative agencies. At first blush, this issue of the reception of legal knowledge might seem too obvious to list specifically as a hypothesis. However, the reason that it is given particular treatment is that there are a number of barriers to the dissemination of legal knowledge within administrative organisations. Two such barriers which emerged from fieldwork are explored in this chapter. First, I look at the issue of the containment of legal knowledge, whereby the structure and routines of an organisation can impede the dissemination of knowledge. Secondly, I explore the relationship between administrative decision-makers and their legal advisors. Before exploring these barriers, however, we must first consider in greater depth the issue of the complexity of organisations and its importance for thinking about the reception of legal knowledge into organisations.

In thinking about the reception of legal knowledge into administrative agencies, it is important to recognise from the outset that such agencies are usually quite complex organisations. This is a fact which is often glossed over for the purposes of judicial review litigation. From the court's perspective, the decision under scrutiny can easily be regarded as having been made by 'the decision-maker'. The complex bureaucracy, the diverse activities of which produced a final decision-outcome, can be imagined as a single entity. The decision-outcome which is the product of multiple pre-decisions can be artificially reduced to a single discrete 'decision'. The social reality, of course, is quite different. A host of bureaucrats have an input into final decision-outcomes. The decision-making process is better conceived as a network of bureaucrats exercising discretion, culminating in a final outcome which is highly contingent on the discretion of multiple actors. As Hawkins (1992) has noted, decisions have histories and discretion should be viewed in serial perspective. A quick glance at the make up and operations of one of the case study housing authorities, Muirfield Council, illustrates this point well.

Structure and Operations of Muirfield Council's Homeless Persons Unit

Muirfield's Homeless Persons Unit contained three principal teams which managed the homeless application process (though others also had an input). The casework team was responsible for determining homeless applications which were referred to it by the assessments and advice team. It investigated homelessness applications and decided what duties, if any, were owed under the Housing Act 1996. The assessments and advice team was responsible for conducting initial assessments in relation to all homeless applications. Assessments and advice officers interviewed all homeless applicants and determined whether referral to the casework team was required. The temporary accommodation section was responsible for providing temporary accommodation following a mandate from the casework team. It also was responsible for transferring homeless people within its temporary accommodation stock, either from one hotel to another or to a temporary house or flat. Each of these teams had an input into final decision outcomes.

Casework Team

Most obviously, the casework team was formally responsible for issuing official decisions to homeless applicants about their claim for housing, though a number of officers could be involved in the process of producing the final decision. Some decisions could be made without the authorisation of a team leader. Where an application was to be rejected for any reason, the caseworker was authorised to do this without prior consultation with his/her team leader. This division of potential decision-outcomes into those requiring team leader authorisation and those which did not was enforced by the computerised decision-letter writing facility. Caseworkers were automatically denied access to 'acceptance' decision-letter templates until a team leader had registered his/her authorisation on the system. Where, however, a caseworker was inclined to accept a housing duty towards the applicant, the ultimate decision had to be made by a team leader. In these cases, when the caseworker felt that enough information had been obtained for the application to be determined, he/she would write a recommendation and pass it with the file to his/her team leader for decision. Although caseworkers adopted their own style for compiling this recommendation, it generally followed the format of giving a brief background and summary of the case, followed by the provision of details under the following headings—'eligibility', 'homelessness', 'priority need', 'intentionality', and 'local connection'. Within each section the caseworker offered an opinion on whether or not the applicant passed these stages of enquiry, and the reasons for the caseworker's findings. The team leader would read the file, then make a decision and hand it back to the caseworker to send the letter and complete other administrative tasks.

However, this simplified image of ultimate decision-making by the team leader belies a more complicated picture on closer inspection whereby the caseworkers were able to use their discretion to impact upon decision outcomes. For example, the drafting of the recommendation was an important site of discretion for the caseworker.

Caseworkers used these recommendations to try and manipulate the team leader into making a decision favoured by them. One caseworker described this process as follows,

> if you're an experienced caseworker, whatever you write will be accepted, basically. There are very few occasions where anything I've sent up [to my team leader] has come back and we've totally disagreed . . . If you're experienced, they tend to trust your judgement so they tend not to question what you write up. I think we all abuse that. They trust me to make the right decision . . . and they won't really look much deeper into it—especially if it is a big case. No-one looks at the whole case file. If you've made all the enquiries, they'll tend to accept the front sheet and look at that. So I think that does swing a lot of cases . . . The way you write it up dictates the way the case was looked at. We all do that . . . It's like writing a story.
>
> (*Caseworker, Muirfield*)

Even within the casework team, then, a number of officers could informally exercise discretion which might impact on final decision outcomes. More formally, however, the assessments and advice team had a role in issuing final decisions. The activities of this team are considered next.

Assessments and Advice Team

This team also had a direct input into the making of final homelessness decisions, though only in certain kinds of application. This team acted as an initial filter in the homelessness decision-making process and rooted out what were notionally regarded as straightforward rejections. All people applying for housing assistance as homeless people were seen by the assessments and advice team. The first issue to be addressed was whether the applicants were eligible for assistance according to their immigration status. Where applicants were deemed to be ineligible, they were referred on to another team. Where eligible, a further assessment was made as to whether they were homeless and in priority need. All applicants deemed by the assessments and advice team to be either not homeless or not in priority need were rejected. If, however, they were thought to be both homeless and in priority need, the case was referred to the casework team for completion.

The quality of decision-making by the assessments and advice team was, however, problematic. There had been a high turnover of staff in this team, many of whom were temporary staff employed through an employment agency. Assessments and advice officers were paid less than their casework colleagues. Although some members of the team were highly qualified, the work of the team in general was often of poor quality. This view was expressed at all levels of the organisational hierarchy. The manager, for example, recognised that there were problems with the team, describing their work as 'a bit "iffy" '. Caseworkers similarly complained about the poor quality of work on receiving a referral from the assessments and advice team. Observation of decision-making with the team confirmed this impression. The work of the assessments and advice team was characterised by the daily struggle to get through the list of applicants waiting to be assessed. The manager recognised that the team was overworked and got rid of a lot of work which the casework team would otherwise have to do. The pressure of work and the need to either move applicants on to the next stage (ie, caseworkers), or to refuse them, informed the character of, and placed constraints upon the extent and quality of officers' casework.

Temporary Accommodation Team

Perhaps surprisingly, the temporary accommodation team also had an input into final decision outcomes, though only indirectly. Shortly before fieldwork commenced, Muirfield introduced a policy that all applicants who required an offer of temporary accommodation were to be offered only one B&B placement (subject to a further offer in exceptional circumstances). If this offer was refused then the case was to be 'discharged'—that is, Muirfield indicated to the applicant that it had exhausted all its duties towards him/her and that no further enquiries were to be made and no further assistance offered. Caseworkers believed that the policy was designed to 'get rid of people'. The manager expressed this differently. For him, the policy was designed to deter those applicants who were not 'literally homeless'. By introducing the policy of making only one offer of temporary accommodation, the manager was attempting to force the hand of homeless applicants. If they were literally homeless and genuinely needed accommodation, so the argument ran, they would take whatever temporary accommodation was offered.

Notwithstanding the different explanations of why the policy was introduced, it was clear that it had an impact on the outcome of some homeless applications, elevating the significance of temporary accommodation allocations and granting power to temporary accommodation officers which was strikingly disproportionate to their formal status within the organisation. This is explained by the fact that the temporary accommodation available to Muirfield was of a highly variable quality. At the time of fieldwork there was an average of over two thousand families/single people in B&B accommodation. Increasingly, Muirfield had to search for hotels further away from its area in order to be able discharge its temporary accommodation duties. This meant that applicants were frequently offered B&B accommodation which was a considerable distance away (occasionally in excess of 20 miles) from Muirfield, and was frequently considered unreasonable by applicants for this reason. In addition, the physical quality of the hotels was a problem for Muirfield. A number of the hotels it used had a pest control problem. During fieldwork a number of them required to be fumigated in order to deal with cockroach infestation. Several of the caseworkers informed me that Muirfield, at the time of fieldwork, was using hotels which it had classed as uninhabitable in previous years.

In light of the combination of Muirfield's one offer policy and the poor quality of much of the temporary accommodation stock, caseworkers took pains to nurture good relationships with the temporary accommodation officers, aware of their power within the overall system. Where caseworkers wanted to secure 'good' temporary accommodation for certain applicants, they would attempt to secure favours from temporary accommodation officers:

> It's based on personalities. If you get on with somebody who's a colleague and you could say to them, 'I need this guy to be in [a particular area] coz he needs to go to the hospital', or whatever, you could actually turn round to them and say 'do us a favour and try and get them in there', and they will do that. Whereas normally you just say 'I want them put in B&B somewhere', and they could go anywhere. They may get lucky and get [a favourable area], they may not. The chances are they'll be placed anywhere. So it does have an influence, if you try to get your client in a particular area . . . Personalities and characters do play a big part in terms of getting you what you want.
>
> (*Caseworker, Muirfield*)

Implications for the Reception of Legal Knowledge

The above brief description of some of the decision-making activities within Muirfield Council highlights the multiple exercises of discretion which are hidden from view behind the formal decision outcome. This has implications for consideration of our first hypothesis. The hypothesis concerning the reception of legal knowledge into the government agency needs further clarification. It is now clear that the conditions which are conducive to compliance with administrative law are where all those who exercise discretion in the run up to the final decision outcome receive the requisite legal knowledge. Judicial review's capacity to secure compliance will be enhanced by the full range of decision-makers receiving legal knowledge, and not just the agency itself. The complete dissemination of legal knowledge, however, can be a difficult task. Rather than being disseminated, it is easy for legal knowledge to be contained within a particular corner of an organisation and it is to this issue that we now turn.

Organisational Complexity and the Containment of Legal Knowledge

The complexity of organisations permits the containment of legal knowledge. Legal knowledge may enter an organisation—often at a senior level—but be contained within a small group of actors without being disseminated throughout the organisation. Daintith and Page in their study of the central government executive, give a number of examples of the dissemination of legal knowledge, including, notably, *The Judge Over Your Shoulder* (Treasury Solicitor's Department, 1995), but nevertheless raise general concerns about the effectiveness of information dissemination across Whitehall (1999: 313). Indeed the point about organisational complexity as a barrier to knowledge dissemination is presumably writ large in relation to central government. In this section we examine the case study of Eastbank Council to illustrate how organisational complexity even within a sub-unit of a relatively small department within a single local authority can create problems for the dissemination of knowledge.

As indicated in chapter 1, most of Eastbank's experiences of judicial review had concerned disputes about intentional homelessness decisions. These decisions were made by a small committee of officers called the 'Intentionality Panel'. The composition of this panel had changed a few times over the years. However, for a number of years prior to fieldwork, the panel comprised the legal manager and an appointed team leader. The panel was a notable point of entry for legal knowledge into Eastbank's homeless persons unit. The decision-making on cases which were scrutinised in judicial review litigation were discussed in this forum. Decisions which were thought vulnerable to litigation were similarly discussed here. And, of course, the aftermath of litigation on intentional homelessness decisions was experienced most directly in this panel and its ongoing decision-making.

It was not just direct experience of litigation, however, that generated legal knowledge. The appointment of the legal manager to the panel was also a source for new legal information and expertise. The legal manager's presence was considered to be particularly significant in developing the character of panel decision-making. She instilled a confidence about legal matters and about defending legal challenges:

> We were housing officers with a little bit of legal. But [with the arrival of the legal manager] there was someone who knows the field, what's going on. Solicitors could turn it round. Words could be used in the wrong place in a sentence because a precedent of X, Y, Z said you can't use that word, and I wouldn't know that. And that's the sort of thing that, with [the legal manager] being there, she could say, 'look, don't put that word in. Let's take this out. Don't write that. Do this and all that.'
>
> (*Manager, Eastbank*)

The legal manager had a similar impression of the change in the panel's decision-making which occurred on her appointment:

> I think at the time they didn't have a lot of confidence in decision-making. The decision-letters were not particularly good in so far as they didn't express reasons—or the reasons given were a couple of lines. I think it was an idea of whoever was in the Town Hall at the time, in the legal services, that they needed someone to sit on this panel—have some legal adviser. They always thought it was a good idea and in fact it was a very good idea. I think it changed their perceptions of what they could do. I think often if they got a solicitor's letter it would be 'Oh gosh, what do we do with this? Let's just accept the family to save a lot of problems.' So it was different when someone came along and said 'What you can do is this . . .', or, 'You can actually deal with it this way . . .', or, 'What you need to do now is this . . .' And so as a result of that and having had some cases that were dealt with I think probably a bit more thoroughly than they otherwise might have done, and having actually gone to court and seeing you actually can win these cases, there seemed to be a change in the way that they dealt with the cases.
>
> (*Legal manager, Eastbank*)

By the beginning of fieldwork, the composition of the panel had changed. The legal manager had left, a new team leader chaired the panel and caseworkers were seconded to it on a rotating basis. However, the fact that the panel had been restricted previously to one team leader and the legal manager was significant to the reception of legal knowledge into Eastbank's homeless persons unit as a whole. Legal knowledge was contained within the panel and not disseminated further. This meant, of course, that it was largely restricted to the single team leader who had dominated the intentionality panel for years. This team leader noted:

> I have an in-depth knowledge of how bad cases went, where we went wrong. I could see what line the opposition would take, from being involved in so many judicial reviews, and we could stop it there and then if we thought we wouldn't get this one through—we'd go again, we'd make another decision. However, even though I'd come back from each case if we did go off to judicial review and I would speak to the officer concerned as to the principle, as to what went wrong, why we won, why we lost, I don't think everyone was getting the benefit of that, coz it would be just that individual and the principal concerned.
>
> *(Team leader, Eastbank)*

The effects of this knowledge containment were apparent within the team as a whole. Although Eastbank had experienced 11 judicial reviews (and a further three cases which had stopped at application for leave stage) over the period of seven and a half years (some of which were significant legal cases from a doctrinal perspective) individual officers in the casework team knew very little indeed about its history of litigation. The most striking example of this concerned another team leader who, in interview, initially claimed that Eastbank had never been subject to judicial review, but then corrected himself, noting that he knew of one case (though he couldn't recall its name). The same was true, although to a lesser degree, with caseworkers. Generally, caseworkers were aware that Eastbank had been involved in judicial review litigation, although none were sure to what extent or what the litigation had been about. Most officers had an awareness of one judicial review case in particular which enjoyed a certain notoriety within the team, though they differed in their understanding of what the case was about—what the legal reasoning and implications of the case were in terms of ongoing decision-making. In general Eastbank's direct experience of judicial review was of little relevance to their routine decision-making:

For years and years [team leader A] was the only senior in this unit who knew anything really about intentionality decisions and how you actually write the letters, how you come to the decisions. It was only [team leader A]. It was only recently, since [team leader B] was appointed, that someone else became involved . . . The knowledge is not shared. You're only told if it's your case. And the rest of the unit don't really know what's gone on and what's happened. They don't even know why [team leader A] is flying out the door to go to court. We're not aware at times. Our communications channels at times are not very good.

(Caseworker, Eastbank)

The existence of the intentionality panel, its membership and the subject matter of judicial review litigation in Eastbank all combined to contain legal information and prevent its dissemination. Of course, legal knowledge can fail to be disseminated for more mundane reasons. Sheer pressure of work can overcome the best of intentions to disseminate legal knowledge. Eastbank also faced this problem. The same team leader described how her intention to share the knowledge that she had gained from handling litigation had been thwarted:

I think I did make a promise that I would start feeding back to the team at quality time session, but since I made that promise I haven't even been there. I will do it. Because it's all being deferred downwards, being pushed downwards, they need to know.

(Team leader, Eastbank)

Similar problems occurred in relation to more general legal information. There was a willingness on the part of the manager and team leaders in Eastbank for caseworkers to be routinely kept up-to-date with legal knowledge and developments and for informal incremental legal training to be part of the professional development of staff. However, certainly during fieldwork, there was little evidence of this actually happening. Caseworkers remarked that they would only 'gen up' on case law developments when they were going for job interviews. The casework team were under tremendous pressure of work. It can be characterised as being trapped in a prolonged state of crisis management. The will to incorporate routine and effective informal legal training was overridden in practice by the straightforward objective of coping with the bureaucratic demands of a heavy and constant workload.

Relationships with Legal Advisors

The second factor which impacts on the extent to which legal knowledge is received into administrative agencies and which emerged from fieldwork, is the nature of the relationship between decision-makers and legal advisors. The stronger the relationship between bureaucrats and their legal advisors, the greater (generally speaking) will be the level of legal knowledge within the agency.

The housing authorities which took part in this study enjoyed different levels of relationship with its legal advisors. Timbergreens had the strongest relationship. Since early 1990, the Homeless Persons Unit had an appointed legal advisor who for a number of years was even a member of the Homeless Persons Unit's management team. This legal advisor had both scheduled and ad hoc contact with Timbergreens' casework team. The relationships between individual caseworkers and the legal advisor were very friendly and familiar to the extent that they would occasionally approach her directly for advice on legal questions. Although this was a practice which was not formally recognised nor condoned, the caseworkers were sufficiently familiar with the legal advisor for this to be an acceptable, albeit, infrequent practice. Team leaders contacted the legal advisor more frequently on an ad hoc basis, although their main point of contact with her was on a scheduled basis (see below). In the main, however, the manager had the most frequent informal contact with the legal advisor with whom he had a close working relationship. The manager regularly consulted her on legal questions relating to the casework team's decision-making on an ad hoc basis. The legal advisor also had scheduled meetings with the team leaders concerning certain cases within their overall workload. A decision that an applicant was intentionally homeless was never made without prior consultation with the legal advisor. Fortnightly meetings were arranged to discuss such cases.

In Eastbank, as we have already noted, the legal manager used to sit on the intentionality panel. When Eastbank was re-arranged into business units, however, this practice ceased as the Homeless Persons Unit would be charged for her services. A similar situation had occurred in Muirfield after its internal reorganisation. There were other reasons, however, for its lack of contact with legal advisors which will be discussed further in relation to legal conscientiousness in chapter 3. Suffice it to say for the time being that Muirfield's homelessness officers regarded themselves as being more expert in the law than their legal advisors. Further, as we shall see in chapter 3, the Homeless Persons' Unit took a robust and confident approach to litigation and regarded its legal advisors as being a little too nervous and prone to panic. As the manager noted:

> I think we'd have more trouble if we had a solicitor's department, like some authorities, that you had to run every intentionality decision through . . . They'd start wanting to cover every single little point so there's no danger, whereas, once the decision's made, someone like [our barrister] can work on it and do a damage limitation.
>
> (*Manager, Muirfield*)

Of course, legal advisors need not only be internal. External advice from barristers or other experts could be sought. One of the advantages of prolonged experiences of judicial review is that relationships with individual barristers can be forged. Timbergreens took advantage of this and was in the habit of receiving occasional training from its barrister. Timbergreens regarded this is as part of its training of officers and another way of disseminating legal information within the unit.

A final barrier to the reception of legal knowledge which has not yet been explored, is that of the agency's attitude to law. Where compliance with law is a low organisational priority, then there is likely to be a parallel lack of effort to disseminate legal information. The question of agencies' attitude to law and its implications for knowledge dissemination is a matter which will be returned to in greater depth in chapter 3 which deals with legal conscientiousness.

3

Legal Conscientiousness

IN CHAPTER 2 we explored the first hypothesis relating to administrative decision-makers about the conditions which will maximise
compliance with administrative law: that the more they receive legal
knowledge from judicial review about what administrative law
requires of them, the greater will judicial review's capacity be to secure
compliance with the law. In this chapter we consider the second
hypothesis relating to the decision-makers: that judicial review's
regulatory capacity will be enhanced by the decision-makers being
conscientious about applying their legal knowledge to the full range of
their routine decision-making tasks.

Knowing what the law requires of you as a decision-maker is not
enough to ensure compliance (Kagan, Gunningham and Thornton,
2003). Decision-makers must also care about acting lawfully. A commitment to legality must be part of the decision-maker's professional
orientation and value system. They must be conscientious about applying their legal knowledge to the full range of their decision-making
tasks. As Bardach and Kagan have noted: 'compliance is problematic
unless there is an underlying attitude of willing co-operation' (1982:
100). This, however, is a tall order.

There is much in the business of routine administrative decision-
making that prevails against legal conscientiousness. In addition to
formal and rival normative systems within the decision-making environment (which are explored in chapter 5), Galligan (2001) has noted
that the instrumental rationalities which drive bureaucracies towards
the goal of efficiency have a habit of organically forming themselves
into normative orders in their own right—'institutions become value-
based, in a way that goes beyond instrumental utility' (2001: 88). He
argues that administrative discretion permits the development of
administrative rationalities which in turn permit the development of
administrative autonomy. The extent to which these are present is
important for our understanding of how difficult it is for legal values
to infiltrate routine decision-making practices. Galligan's point is
that administrative organisations organically produce internal

normative systems in relation to which legal values are unwelcome intruders.

The data from fieldwork offered clear examples of such internal normative ordering which was resistant to legal influence. These are discussed below and relate to the use of what I term 'professional intuition' and a prevailing culture of suspicion relating to the honesty of applicants. As we will see, these characteristics of routine casework decision-making reveal strong internal demands about what the 'right' decision is and about how to reach it—demands that are independent of, and often in conflict with legal values about how the decision-making process should unfold. They demonstrate that the decision-makers, to a greater or lesser degree, lacked legal conscientiousness. They did not care about applying their legal knowledge to their decision-making routines because they lacked faith in law to produce the right outcome. This last point will be developed further below. First, however, we turn to a discussion of professional intuition.

PROFESSIONAL INTUITION

A central characteristic of the homelessness decision-making observed was that of 'professional intuition'. By this I mean that decision-makers had developed a confidence in their ability to gain an almost immediate sense of the truth underlying an applicant's claim for housing. By virtue of their experience, they felt able to 'just know' what a case was about—what Hawkins calls 'axiomatic decision-making' (2002: 427). As one caseworker from Eastbank noted:

> With most cases I know what to do. I know exactly what to do and I know largely what the decision is going to be. After you've conducted an interview with an applicant, most of the time you know whether that's a rejection or an approval. You have to do your routine investigations. Basically I find my investigations confirm what your feelings are at the end of an appointment. So, once you're experienced you know whether this is going to be an approval or a rejection.

(Caseworker, Eastbank)

This was a skill which was learned on the job and so was reproduced and perpetuated within the organisation. Professional intuition is a natural by-product of the routinisation of decision-making which has been observed in other discretionary contexts (Waegel, 1981; Emerson, 1983; Lempert, 1992). Loveland (1995) discusses 'intuitive techniques' employed by housing officers in his study of homelessness decision-making to determine the truth of applicants' accounts in the absence of corroborative sources,

> all three councils seemed prepared informally to adjust their decision-making procedures in response to officers' intuitive feelings about the potential 'deviance' of particular applicants. (1995: 156)

Cowan (1997) also discusses a similar finding in relation to homelessness cases where the applicant claimed she was fleeing domestic violence. He reports that the 'gut feeling' of the applicant's genuineness was central to the determination of the application. It is suggested that 'intuitive techniques' go further and are more central to the character of much decision-making. Indeed, casework can be fashioned around the substantiation of the decision-maker's intuitive sense of the right outcome.

Professional intuition was evidenced most clearly in relation to intentional homelessness cases, particularly where the caseworker sensed that the applicant was trying to conceal the truth about this. Casework would then be characterised by the attempt to expose the truth in order to be able to secure a legally defensible 'intentionally homeless' decision. There is an irony in the fact that such professional intuition which portrays the applicant as lying in order to circumvent the obstacles to a 'not intentionally homeless' decision, in turn drove caseworkers to carry out casework aimed at overcoming a different set of obstacles which stood in the way of an 'intentionally homeless' decision. A picture emerges of both parties trying to outsmart the other. One of the team leaders who had previously worked as a caseworker expressed it in terms of a competition between the officer and the applicant:

> There's a competitiveness, I think, between us and them, them being applicants—not your ordinary applicant, but if somebody is likely to get a negative decision and is always lying, there is a determination to root out the truth. And that's quite an enjoyable exercise. I think most people would find that enjoyable—the sleuth part.
>
> (*Team leader, Timbergreens*)

CULTURE OF SUSPICION

Professional intuition, as already noted above, is organisationally produced and reflects organisational culture. An aspect of organisational culture which was displayed very strongly in all three field sites and informed professional intuition and consequent casework related to the decision-makers' role as a gatekeeper to resources. A general culture of suspicion existed in relation to the openness and truthfulness of homelessness applicants. This might also be described as a siege mentality, whereby the homeless persons units were being subjected to bogus applications. This was reflected in how caseworkers interpreted applicants' behaviour in interviews. In Eastbank, for example, one caseworker indicated that she was very suspicious of applicants who cried during interviews: 'If they start to cry before you've even said anything, they've got something to hide.' This remark was made at the end of an interview in case E9. The applicant was a Nigerian woman with a new-born baby who had been refused assistance the previous day on the grounds that she did not have recourse to public funds. She was tearful as she recounted her story which involved her husband in Nigeria having married a second wife because she had not borne him a son and her having had to send some of her daughters to America because she could not support them.

The culture of suspicion was also reflected in doubting the honesty of applicants' accounts of their circumstances. In each field site a widespread view was held that applicants told lies in order to circumvent the legal barriers which prevented them from being offered housing. The belief was that applicants learned how to 'play the game' when making a homelessness application—that they became aware of how to fill in applications and answer interview questions in order to secure an offer of housing. For example, in Timbergreens, in case T56, the caseworker explained after an initial interview that 'it's a straightforward case unless he gets wise and introduces something else.' Another caseworker from Timbergreens remarked that it was amazing how, as 'stock questions' in interviews had changed over the years, so had the 'stock answers' given by applicants, adding, 'a lot of priming goes on in the [Southern Asian] community.'

Indeed, the culture of suspicion rested in part on ethnic stereotyping (see Halliday, 2000b) or in relation to immigrants. In Eastbank, for example, there was evidence of an organisational perception, particularly in relation to asylum seekers, that the homelessness system was being abused and that they were attempting to take advantage of the casework team. In case E145, for example, the applicant was a recent asylum seeker from Somalia. The applicant had been booked into B&B after a preliminary interview. His claim of homelessness was based on being asked to leave a friend's home. The friend had attended the offices to confirm this. His priority need rested on his claim that his niece, also recently arrived from Somalia, was dependant on him. The niece was registered as the applicant's dependent for the purposes of social security benefits. However, on a second interview, another case-worker terminated the B&B booking on the ground that she was not satisfied that the applicant was homeless or in priority need. The case-worker was convinced that the applicant was lying. She had spotted a number of inconsistencies in the applicant's story (told via an inter-preter): according to Home Office papers concerning the niece, the applicant was not the 'sponsor' of the child. Rather, the sponsor was the person who was making the applicant homeless ('the excluder'). The applicant had also indicated the wrong port of entry for the niece. During the interview the previous day, the applicant had said that he had collected the niece from port of entry X, but had been corrected in interview by the niece. Another indicator of the applicant's deceit in the perception of the caseworker was the fact that he had made an error in giving the niece's date of birth. Further, the caseworker had quizzed the applicant about the colour of the wallpaper in the excluder's home. When the applicant was unable to answer, this further fuelled the belief that the application was a sham. The caseworker believed that the applicant had not been excluded from his friend's home and that the girl was not in fact dependent on the applicant and that his claim to such was a ruse to obtain housing.

The caseworker set two conditions to be satisfied before the applicant could be reinstated into B&B: first, the excluder had to attend the offices and provide proof of both the exclusion and his right to exclude; second, the applicant had to obtain and show confirmation from the Home Office that it was satisfied that the applicant was indeed the 'sponsor' of the niece. The caseworker indicated that the above conditions were 'just delaying tactics' and recognised that Eastbank was on 'dodgy legal grounds'. However, she felt resolute in her course of action because she was convinced the applicant was lying, noting 'he can tell a yarn—he's worse than a lawyer . . . He's obviously lying and we've got to get tough in cases like this. There's collusion to get priority, to get housing'.

Because the applicant was unable to fulfil the conditions, B&B was refused again. The following week, however, the applicant returned with a sworn affidavit stating that his niece was dependent on him. At this point the team leader decided that B&B could not be withheld any longer. The caseworker was disappointed but philosophical, saying, 'I'm not a immigration officer. You win some, you lose some.'

The interesting point here is that the 'inconsistencies' in the applicant's account were seized upon by the caseworker as being signifiers of deceit and collusion. It did not seem possible for these 'inconsistencies' to have alternative explanations—that the applicant made a mistake about his niece's date of birth; that he was mistaken about which port of entry he had collected his niece from; that the Home Office operated to a different set of concepts and procedures which do not easily translate to housing provision matters; that subtleties may have been lost in translation; that the dependency of a child could have changed over time; that the homelessness system is sufficiently complex that non-English speaking new asylum seekers might have had considerable difficulties in knowing how to circumvent it; and so on. Of the possible explanations available to the caseworker, the culture of suspicion appeared to lead to a restrictive one which fitted with the general siege mentality. Casework then took the form of trying to find a fit for this restrictive explanation. The caseworker here was trying to prove collusion, an attempt, on this occasion, in which she didn't succeed.

The case of E145, in addition to offering an example of how a culture of suspicion manifests itself in the interpretation of applicant's accounts, also demonstrates that the homeless persons units adopted tactics to counter what they believed to be bogus applications—in that case, the suspension of temporary accommodation and the requirement of a high level of independent corroboration of the applicant's story. Other tactics, however, were observed. In Timbergreens, the casework team employed a tactic of 'information bingeing'—getting as much information from applicants as early as possible in order to counter the story-changing practices of applicants. Timbergreen's legal advisor noted:

> We make decisions based on what is known at the time. Applicants often change their story after they've been to a solicitor. [Timbergreens] takes a stand on this. The first interview is probably the most honest account you'll get.
>
> (*Legal advisor, Timbergreens*)

Further defensive tactics of Timbergreens are considered below in relation to their use of legal knowledge to protect themselves from judicial scrutiny. First, however, a brief word must be said about understanding the culture of suspicion which was evident (to greater or lesser degrees) in each field site and which informed much of the decision-making practices.

Understanding a Culture of Suspicion

The culture of suspicion, no doubt more prevalent in front-line decision-making, might be explained as a means by which decision-makers cope with the difficulty of the decision-making task. Lipsky (1980) has noted the alienating effects of street-level bureaucratic work. Treating the claimant as one of a category rather than as an individual compromises the ability of the worker to treat the person fully as a human. Front-line workers, then, develop coping-mechanisms to alleviate the alienating aspects of their work. Coping with the demands of people in extreme circumstances and making decisions about whether to house them—and often having to refuse—is unquestionably a very difficult and stressful task. One of the most interesting themes in Lipsky's important work is the dehumanising disappointment experienced by street-level bureaucrats who enter the field with the image of their work as helping others, only to find that they must serve their bureaucratic goals, rather than their initial humanistic and altruistic ideals. There is a sense of powerlessness about their relationship to the organisation. This was certainly reflected in many of the caseworkers observed, many of whom were left-leaning welfare-oriented workers—very 'human' people making what some might observe as rather inhuman decisions. As one of Muirfield's caseworkers noted, the job had made him into a person that he did not like. The portrayal of (at least some) applicants as cheats is perhaps one way of managing the stress involved in performing the duty of deciding who should be granted assistance— a form of denial of the kinds of decisions that are being made (see Cohen, 2001). It is more human and palatable to refuse help to the bogus or undeserving, as opposed to the needy.

Nevertheless, the culture of suspicion is also an example of a strong internal culture which resists interference from legal values. This point is developed further below.

CREATIVE COMPLIANCE AND A LACK OF FAITH IN LAW

Lacking Faith in Law to Produce the Right Decision

Internal decision-making characteristics like professional intuition and siege mentalities reveal a lack of faith in law's ability to provide the right decision outcome. Rather than looking to law to guide them about how to conduct the decision-making process, decision-makers often start with an intuitive sense of what the outcome should be and fashion the decision-making process around substantiating that objective. The legal requirements of good administration may, on occasion, coincide with this process, but often it does not. What is significant here for our purposes is that decision-makers, in trusting their professional intuition and in reacting out of a siege mentality, reject the normative authority of law. Legality, as an external normative system, has failed in such instances to penetrate and take hold of the internal administrative value system.

Of course, a contrast between judicial review and co-operative approaches to regulatory enforcement gives further insight into the barriers to legal conscientiousness. This was the method adopted by Hertogh (2001) in his study of the operations of the Ombudsman and the administrative courts in the Netherlands. He has made the point that the court's inability to engage in persuasion and dialogue precludes the development of shared understandings and sensibilities and severely curtails its impact on bureaucracies. Indeed, this insight suggests the paradox that the process of judicial review litigation may well curtail the development of a faith in law on the part of administrative decision-makers to provide the right decision outcome. Decision-makers' perceptions about the ability of judges to understand administrative settings and, consequently, their competence to rule on administrative propriety may be an integral part of a faith in law. Where there is a perceived gulf between the decision-makers' and a court's comprehension of the 'reality' of administrative decision-making, legal conscientiousness is likely to be thin. A number of factors may be significant in establishing such a gap. The customary separation between the decision-makers and the resolution of a dispute about a particular case in the process of litigation is surely one such factor. The individual judicial review case is often taken out of the hands of decision-makers and put into the hands of solicitors and thence to barristers in court. The clinical removal of the dispute from the administrative arena leaves little room for the development of shared understandings or sympathetic appreciations of each others' roles. This process lacks much of the intimacy associated with co-operative approaches to enforcement.

Avoiding Legal Control

However, to suggest that there is much in the routine business of administration and in the process of judicial review litigation that militates against a faith in law, is not to say that law is irrelevant to decision-making. On the contrary, the decision-makers in this study were well aware of the power of law through judicial review to obstruct some of their decision-making aims. Indeed, their experiences of being subject to judicial review was very useful in educating them how to creatively comply with the law so as to avoid legal control, a point noted by Daintith and Page in their discussion of creative compliance in executive decision-making in Whitehall (1999: 345–46). In the sections below we identify three methods used to avoid legal control which emerged from fieldwork.

Abusing Legal Process

Timbergreens used its legal knowledge of the litigation process to avoid legal control in relation to the provision of temporary accommodation. The homelessness legislation gave local authorities a duty to provide temporary accommodation to some homeless applicants while their application was being processed:

> If a local authority has reason to believe that an applicant may be homeless and have a priority need, they shall secure that accommodation is made available for his occupation pending a decision they may make as a result of their enquiries.
>
> (Housing Act 1985, s 63(1))

It was quite common, however, for a decision about priority need to take one to two weeks to process. This was necessary where an assessment about the health of the applicant was made by a medical advisor, or where the opinion of an external agency was sought. The practice of the casework team in this situation was to refuse temporary accommodation to such applicants despite the terms of the legislation.

For example in case T9, the applicant was a single man. He had made a homeless application to Timbergreens one month previously. The decision issued in relation to this previous application was that he was homeless but not in priority need. Subsequent to this previous application he had sought advice from a local law centre. When he came back, he brought a letter from the law centre, a psychiatrist's report and a copy of his medical notes. The applicant was very subdued and slow to respond during the interview. He had difficulty in answering basic questions. For example, the caseworker asked him 'What kind of benefits are you on?', and 'Do you have any medical problems?'. To both questions he muttered 'Don't know'. The psychiatrist had indicated in her report that the applicant was suffering from a depressive illness. The solicitor from the law centre indicated that the applicant may have mild learning difficulties. The caseworker told the applicant at the end of the interview that the psychiatrist's report would be sent to Muirfield's medical advisor in the following week so that this advisor could make an assessment of his medical condition. Until the outcome of this medical assessment, however, no temporary accommodation could be offered.

The manager of Muirfield's homeless persons unit was aware that such refusals of temporary accommodation were in breach of his legal duty. The reason he gave for doing so was that it was a way of cutting down on the cost of temporary accommodation provided to homeless families. Temporary accommodation expenditure constituted a very large part of his budget and it was his responsibility to control expenditure within the limits set by the annual budget. He felt able to make such decisions, however, without risking legal sanction,

> if someone did kick up a fuss, then the easy option is to give them a decision-letter saying 'You are not vulnerable', let them challenge that, but in the meantime a recommendation from whoever hopefully would had come through. You can quash the first decision and make a second decision. Even if it's exactly the same, you then can't be challenged on the first decision. The challenge would had been 'It's an incorrect decision because you hadn't taken into account the other party's recommendations.' Well, the second decision will have done. There is therefore no challenge.
>
> (*Manager, Timbergreens*)

Creative Compliance?

It is perhaps a moot point whether or not we should describe the above practice as 'creative compliance'. In their classic article, McBarnet and Whelan describe creative compliance as using the law to escape legal control without violating legal rules . . . [the] *post hoc* manipulation of law to turn it—no matter what the intentions of legislators or enforcers—to the service of their own interests and to avoid unwarranted control. (1991: 848)

Their interests were in exposing the vulnerability of law in formalist form to manipulation by the regulated population. The imagination and legal skills of the regulated population—companies avoiding tax liability in McBarnet and Whelan's study—permitted them to evade legal control because of the form in which the law was expressed. Timbergreens' practices described above are different in two respects. First, the manager certainly believed that he was violating a legal rule, though he did so without risk of legal sanction. The procedural realities of judicial review litigation (which he knew well) permitted him to 'correct' his violation and so render his decision-making process as a whole lawful. He was, in this sense, violating a legal rule without acting unlawfully—at least by the time of potential judicial scrutiny. Secondly, he was not so much manipulating formalist law, as abusing the necessary time delay between rule violation and judicial scrutiny. It was the legal process that was being manipulated rather than the content of the law itself.[1] Nevertheless, regardless of whether one wishes to call it 'creative compliance', it is certainly clear that legal knowledge was being used to avoid legal control, and this practice testifies to the power of competing normative systems within the administrative system which resist the influence of law.

Bullet Proofing Decisions

Another method of avoiding legal control used by the housing authorities was what Sunkin and Le Sueur (1991) have called 'bullet proofing' (see also Bridges, Game and Lomas, 1987). This is a practice whereby government agencies use legal knowledge to immunise their decisions against potential judicial scrutiny. Their knowledge of administrative law and experiences of judicial review allow them to anticipate legal challenge, identify potential vulnerabilities and protect their decisions in the planning process. Each of the housing authorities in this study noted that their experiences of judicial review had taught them the importance of articulating their decisions carefully and demonstrating

---

[1] For further evidence of how procedural realities may be exploited by government agencies, securing only pyrrhic victories for applicants, see Dotan (1999).

the factors which they had 'considered' in the course of decision-making. The manager of Timbergreens, for example, noted:

> We were learning from things that happened in court. If something was criticised in court, (maybe the way a report was worded or the accent of a wording of a letter, or certain documents not being on the file, or something not having been checked) that was all picked up and then relayed back to us, so that we knew in future you must put *this* word in, or you must put *that* sentence in, or *that* document must be available, *this* must be put to the applicant. So the procedures were developing a lot more because of the court cases . . . So that meant a lot of changes that way, from an administrative point of view. So the letters we were sending out became a lot more complicated . . . It also altered some of the things we did—we're not operating now the same way we did 20 years ago, but I think a lot of the difference was on the recording of what we were doing and everybody became a lot more aware of the fact that you had to be seen to have done something. It was simply not good enough to say 'well I discussed this with an applicant', or, 'I did ask them about this'. That was not good enough. You've got to be able to show—'we discussed this. This was the person's response. This was the conversation . . .' When you have a problem during a court case it'll be because it's not recorded . . . So what we were saying to people was 'the things you do *must* be recorded.'
>
> (*Team Leader, Timbergreens*)

Indeed, it was this concern that in part led to the practice of information bingeing already described above. Timbergreens, like the other housing authorities, was concerned to be able to demonstrate that it had considered all the relevant factors in an applicant's case. Indeed, as we shall see below, in some cases it collected information by rote, regardless of the applicant's circumstances, according to a list of interview questions that was routinely supplemented with each experience of judicial review. The important thing to note here is that there was no necessary connection between the information obtained, the demonstration of the 'factors' considered, and the reason for the decision made. The practice of information bingeing and the religious recitation in decision letters of factors considered was largely driven by the desire to avoid legal control, rather than by a commitment to legality.

Pre-empting the Creative Tactics of 'Bogus' Applicants

We noted above in our discussion of the culture of suspicion that agencies imagine themselves to be in a siege situation where applicants attempt creatively to abuse the law in order to secure offers of housing.

Timbergreens employed other defensive practices aimed at neutralising such tactics. One example relates to pre-empting the attempts of unsuccessful applicants to get round an initial refusal by making a second, more creative, application.

One counter-tactic employed by Timbergreens relates to the decision about how to categorise the situation where more than one adult approached it for help as homeless people—whether to class them as joint applicants, or to class one of them as the applicant and the other(s) as dependant(s) of the applicant. Although caseworkers indicated that ultimately this could be the decision of the applicant(s) rather than Timbergreens, in practice the decision was made by the caseworker and was generally not challenged by the applicant(s). Effectively, unless the individuals seeking assistance actively objected to the decision about who was to be treated as the applicant, the decision was one for Timbergreens to make. For example, one caseworker explained that she normally said to the applicants when conducting duty interviews, 'OK, we'll make this a joint application.' She would only alter this position if they objected. The reason for this practice was explained by another caseworker. He explained that Timbergreens had been 'caught out' some years previously when the partner of a sole applicant who had been deemed to be intentionally homeless applied subsequently in her own right, claiming that she had not acquiesced in her husband's actions on which the decision of intentionality was based. Accordingly, the officer explained, the casework team 'like to do them together.' This was done so that, should a wife make a subsequent application claiming that she had no part in the activities on which the first refusal was based, Timbergreens would be able to base a defensible second refusal on the basis of the wife's status as joint applicant in the original application. By making both partners to a relationship joint applicants, Timbergreens felt that it would be able to defensibly refute the credibility of any subsequent claims of one partner that she could not be tied to the intentionality of her homelessness.

THE RELATIONSHIP BETWEEN LEGAL CONSCIENTIOUSNESS AND LEGAL KNOWLEDGE

Having set out what we mean by legal conscientiousness, and observed the considerable administrative pressures which militate against it, we can pause at this stage and return to our discussion in the previous chapter about the potential relationship between a lack of legal conscientiousness and a corresponding lack of legal knowledge. Where an organisation cares little about applying legal knowledge to their decision-making tasks, it is possible that they similarly care little about disseminating legal knowledge. This was evidenced in the case study of Muirfield Council.

Muirfield as a whole took a restrictive approach to homelessness decision-making. Its practice was that if an argument could be made to refuse assistance to applicants, then a refusal should be made. Of the three housing authorities which took part in the study, Muirfield was the most experienced in defending judicial review litigation. It had an easy confidence about itself and was particularly untroubled by the prospect of judicial review. From the point of view of senior officers within the casework team, it was not seen in any way as a threat. The manager had an unrestricted ability to defend proceedings and would do so on every occasion as a matter of policy. There were no financial restrictions on litigation. The cost did not come from within his budget,

> it comes from legal. Legal is not a cost that we've got any control over. We don't even know what each case costs. We don't see the bills. If Muirfield wants us to continue being pretty rigid with them it has to realise that the consequence of that is being challenged in the courts. If it says you can only spend £50K on legal fees, then there's going to come a point when we're going to backtrack on decisions when people threaten us with [litigation].
>
> (*Manager, Muirfield*)

Further, the manager's experiences of litigation over the years had given him confidence in the ability to solve problems after the event,

> it is so stacked against the applicant that when the barrister draws up an affidavit and puts down what you were actually thinking when you made that decision, it just can get you out of so many things that maybe you didn't think of, that you always thought that you could justify almost any decision that you made . . . [W]e won most of the cases, not because we're brilliant, but because, one, it's stacked against them, and, two, we've got a good barrister . . . Maybe the only lesson [we've learned] was that it's worth running with things and not backing off. Because we're always willing to push a point and nobody stops us, we've used it to our benefit.
>
> (*Manager, Muirfield*)

Muirfield had a small legal library, an initiative of a caseworker with a particular interest in law. This housed, among other publications, the

Housing Law Reports. These reports contained the published judgments of cases in which Muirfield had been involved. However, there was no systematic recording or collecting of the judgments of Muirfield's judicial reviews. Officers who attended court might discuss the case with colleagues, and information was passed informally, but the texts of judgments, once passed down from the court, were not routinely given to the Homeless Persons Unit by the legal section. Although some officers expressed a desire to formally discuss cases, or to receive distributed summaries of judgments, this had not been adopted as standard practice at the time of fieldwork. In general, there was no formal attempt to inform current decision-making practice with previous experience of judicial reviews. This was demonstrated clearly in the case of M97.

The applicant in case M97 had given up accommodation abroad and moved with her child to the UK in the hope of finding work. After some time she obtained employment and a child carer for her children. However, the child carer left the applicant's employ and the applicant could not find a replacement. Accordingly, she herself gave up her job to look after her children. During this time she had been living with a friend. Eventually, she had to leave this accommodation. At this point she applied to Muirfield whose officers decided that she was intentionally homeless for having given up her accommodation abroad. She applied for judicial review and was granted leave to do so. Although the decision had been made prior to fieldwork, the judicial review hearing occurred during it and I was able to attend court, observe proceedings, read the case file and discuss the case with the caseworker and team leader who had been involved in the case.

The legal issue was complex and concerned whether the applicant had been unaware of a relevant fact. The applicant argued that the relevant fact was that, in giving up the overseas accommodation and moving to the UK, she would obtain employment and child care, and a replacement of child care if required. If the court was prepared to regard this as a 'relevant fact', and hold that the applicant was unaware of it, then Muirfield would have been wrong to have decided that she was intentionally homelessness. The court held that it could not be regarded as a relevant fact and dismissed the judicial review application.

What was significant about case M97 was that Muirfield had been involved in two cases involving the same legal issue and similar scenarios within the previous 16 months. The second of the judicial review cases had taken place only four months prior to Muirfield's decision in M97. The judgments in these prior cases came to separate conclusions on the question of what is a 'relevant fact'. The judge in M97 noted that previous cases did not 'speak with one voice'. These cases were debated and discussed at some length in court as being directly relevant to case M97 and were referred to in M97's judgment. However, there was no mention of, or reference to these cases in the homelessness file of M97. Despite the fact that Muirfield's barrister debated their content in court, there was no evidence that either of these judgments had been consulted or considered at any point in the decision-making process. There was no attempt to rationalise the conflicting previous judgments, or to decide which was more persuasive. Indeed, apart from one of the judgments having been published in the *Housing Law Reports* (and therefore routinely held as part of these reports for the mini-library), the casework team did not hold the texts of the judgments.

Muirfield's weak legal conscientiousness contributed to its lack of legal knowledge. In case M97, the failure to apply directly relevant legal knowledge to decision-making was not the product of a failure to disseminate the legal knowledge in the first place. Rather, it was the other way round. The legal knowledge was not disseminated because Muirfield did not care about applying it to ongoing decision-making. There was no formal mechanism for attempting to incorporate Muirfield's own (substantial) case law into its future decision-making and such a task, in practice, was irrelevant to the administration of homelessness law. Muirfield relied confidently on its barrister to carry out this kind of task in court after the event, and experience had shown that judicial reviews would normally be successfully defended. The lack of attention to recent, relevant and direct experience of case law was in keeping with Muirfield's restrictive approach to casework. Legal technicalities could be sorted, if necessary, after the event by a capable barrister.

CONCLUSION

In this chapter we have continued our analysis of the decision-makers by examining the notion of legal conscientiousness and noting its importance for increasing judicial review's effectiveness in securing compliance with administrative law. Having set it out as the subject of our second hypothesis, we noted that there is much in the routine business of decision-making which militates against the existence of legal conscientiousness. Further, we suggested that the process of judicial review may, paradoxically, operate to reduce a faith in law to produce the right decision-outcome. Instead, a knowledge of law and the litigation process may be used creatively to avoid legal control.

We will have cause to return to our discussion of legal conscientiousness in the concluding chapter when we will consider whether legal conscientiousness, which our study of homelessness administration suggested is important to compliance with administrative law, will similarly be important in other fields of government administration where decision-making is not made routinely nor on a grand scale. However, for the time being we may conclude this chapter by noting that the combination of legal knowledge and legal conscientiousness is still insufficient to create the full conditions for the maximisation of administrative law compliance through judicial review litigation. Our discussion of the decision-makers must continue by focusing on the matter of legal competence in conscientiously applying legal knowledge to decision-making tasks. This is the subject of chapter 4.

4

Legal Competence

T HIS CHAPTER COMPLETES our exploration of the conditions relating to the decision-makers which will maximise compliance with
administrative law. The final hypothesis to be considered is as follows:
the more decision-makers can derive general principles from specific
judicial review judgments, and then apply these general principles to
relevant specific decision-making tasks within their remit, the greater
will be the effectiveness of judicial review in securing compliance with
administrative law.

So far, in thinking about the reception of legal knowledge into
administrative organisations, I have been treating legal knowledge in a
straightforward fashion, almost as if it was a physical object that was
being passed from one person to another. The reality, of course, is
more complicated and in this section we must divert our attention
towards the question of the *interpretation* of law by administrative
organisations. Legal knowledge only becomes such after a process of
interpretation on the part of the decision-makers. There may be,
however, something of an interpretive gap between the courts and the
administration. As Canon has noted (2004), what the court proclaims
is not always the same as what a government agency understands.
However, compliance with administrative law is being used here to
mean compliance with what the *courts* understand to be the meaning
and implications of law, rather than with how the administrative
decision-makers interpret it. The basic premise of this section is that
compliance with administrative law will be greatest when the government agency and the courts share an understanding about what the law
means and requires.

Once again, however, it is important to note that this is a tall order.
There is a great deal that stands in the way of such interpretive synergy
between the courts and the administration. The discussion which
follows is divided into three sections. First, I consider the relational
distance between the courts and government agencies and the limited
room for dialogue. Secondly, I consider, by reference to fieldwork data,
what might be described as the 'bureaucratic' application of legal

knowledge and the difficulties this poses for the achievement of interpretive synergy. Thirdly, I consider, again from fieldwork data, the
bounded application of legal knowledge to decision-making tasks.

RELATIONAL DISTANCE BETWEEN THE COURTS AND
THE ADMINISTRATION

Relational distance is a concept which has been used in the regulation
literature to think about the impact of the intimacy of relationships
between regulators and regulatees on enforcement practices. The idea
(much simplified) is that the greater the intimacy, the less formal sanctions will be relied upon. Instead, more informal processes of persuasion and negotiation will take place, as is characteristic of more
intimate relationships. Various hypotheses developed out of this basic
notion have been tested in a variety of settings (see, for example
Grabosky and Braithwaite, 1986; Hood et al, 1999).

The concept of relational distance, however, may also be helpful
for us in thinking about the interpretive gap between the courts and
the administration, and the difficulties in closing it. We have already
noted in chapter 3, in thinking about the significance of legal conscientiousness to compliance, that there is no room for the co-operative
practices of persuasion and negotiation in relation to the judicial
review of administrative action. Sossin (2004) has suggested that soft
law may provide a conduit for dialogue between the administration
and the courts. By reading soft law instruments, the judiciary may
well learn things about the social reality of administrative decision-
making. But this is hardly the same thing as the kind of dialogue
envisaged in, for example, Black's image of conversational regulation
(1997). This has implications for how government agencies interpret
the law.

Interpretive Communities and Compliance

Black (1997) has offered important insights into the importance
of interpretive communities to effective regulation. She notes, for
example, the inadequacy of detailed regulation to the securing of
compliance with regulatory standards (see also Bardach and Kagan,
1982). She argues that detailed regulations are an attempt to mimic the

background taken-for-granted interpretive schema which exist within interpretive communities and which give rise to settled meanings:

> Increasing precision . . . is an attempt to substitute rules for the tacit under-standings and informed reading which rules need, but which may not exist. As such it can only fail: increased precision may reduce but can never elimi-nate the inherent indeterminacy of rules and does not in the end create the understanding which it is trying to replace. (1997: 217)

Shared understandings about the meaning and implications of law, then, can exist within interpretive communities. But effort is required to build and foster such communities. Education and training is impor-tant (Black, 1997: 245). Dialogue, above all, is essential (Black, 1998). The process of judicial review does little to bring government agencies and the courts within the same interpretive community, as Hertogh's work (2001) confirms. Internal knowledge dissemination systems, as discussed already in chapter 2, can help to close the gap. Relationships with legal advisors may also assist—they might take on a role akin to internal compliance officers in Parker's terms (1999b). Further, in the field of homelessness law, there is some evidence that the introduction of the statutory internal review scheme has some educative potential (Cowan and Halliday, 2003: chapter 4). However, it seems clear that the ideal of interpretive synergy between the courts and government agencies is quite elusive given the substantial separation and lack of dialogue between the two.

This is not to suggest, of course, that all legal matters are doomed to alternative 'administrative' interpretations. Some questions of law are clearer—or more settled than others, and so interpretation is less of an issue. However, there is sufficient room for alternative understandings within the province of administrative law to make this point signifi-cant. As Sunkin (2004) notes, there is no single hard-edge separating judicial review and administration, and we must pay attention as socio-legal scholars to government agencies' interpretations and re-interpretations of the messages emanating from the courts.

The ability of the agencies to understand law and its implications in the terms shared by the courts is an aspect of what I term 'legal competence'. A second, and closely related aspect of legal competence concerns how agencies seek to apply legal knowledge to their decision-making tasks. This is a matter to which we now turn.

BUREAUCRATIC APPLICATION OF LEGAL KNOWLEDGE

Julia Black has captured the tension for regulatory effectiveness between substantive compliance with regulatory goals and formally rational compliance with regulatory rules:

> Of themselves [precise rules] do not represent overall quality, they are simply measurable proxies for it, and may indeed serve to undermine it: promoting or facilitating the mechanical and unthinking compliance that it may have been the aim of the purposive rule to override. This tension between achieving a high quality of conduct and enabling enforcement perhaps presents the tension between formalism and substantiveness in a different guise, one not of bureaucratic rationality, but of regulatory effectiveness. (1997: 222)

This insight parallels the problem which the bureaucratic application of legal knowledge poses for maximum compliance with administrative law. There is an inevitable degree of tension between the bureaucratic mode of legal knowledge application and full compliance with administrative law. Administrative law's standards of good administration exist at quite a high level of generality and are best regarded as being broad purposive principles of general application. The bureaucratic mode of operation, however, is formally rational. It drags the principles of administrative law down from a high level of generality and fixes them to the specific in terms of precise rules which can be followed by bureaucrats. This is how the bureaucratic goal of efficiency is achieved. The legally conscientious bureaucratic response to judicial review, then, is to translate legal knowledge into detailed rules. However, this misses the purposive general nature of administrative law. To borrow a metaphor from Black, the typical bureaucratic response risks not being able to see the wood for the trees (1997: 219).

The case study of Timbergreens illustrates the bureaucratic response to legal knowledge gained from judicial review.

Case Study of Timbergreens

Timbergreens was perhaps the most formally rational operation of the three case studies. Each homelessness application which was received was categorised by a team leader according to an internally generated typology of cases set out opposite:

A: Possibly Intentionally Homeless—settlement grounds
where the team leader thinks that a decision of intentional homelessness
is possible for 'settlement reasons' (see below).

B: Possibly Intentionally Homeless—non-settlement grounds
where the team leader thinks that a decision of intentional homelessness
is possible for reasons other than 'settlement' ones.

C: Referral of housing duty to another local authority
where a duty to secure accommodation exists but Timbergreens intends
to refer the duty to another local authority.

D: Medical (1 bed)
where the applicant requires only a one-bedroomed property and medical
information is required to determine the case.

E: Social problems/medical problems/special circumstances
where the applicant has special needs and a care in the community report
is required to determine his housing requirements.

G: Management transfer
where an existing tenant of Timbergreens is to be rehoused on management grounds and is staying in temporary accommodation pending the
availability of suitable accommodation.

H: Dodgy/more information needed
where more information is required to be able to properly categorise the
case, *or* where it is felt that the applicant may not be telling the truth.

I: Straightforward case
where only minimal enquiries are required to make a decision to accept a
duty to secure accommodation for the applicant and it thought likely that
a decision to accept a duty will be made.

J: Referral of housing duty from another local authority
where another local authority is referring the duty to secure accommodation to Timbergreens.

K: Did not turn up
where an applicant was placed into temporary accommodation but did
not turn up there.

L: Asylum seekers
where the applicant is an asylum seeker who is entitled to assistance under
the homelessness legislation.

Some of the these terms require further explanation. Both 'A' and 'B' cases were classified as being 'possibly intentionally homeless cases'. These were generally referred to as 'possible intentionals' or, more often, as 'PIH' cases. The phrase 'possibly intentionally homeless' originated from within the casework team—it was not part of the legislation or homelessness case law. When a case was deemed to be a 'PIH' case, it meant that the caseworker was put on notice that the team leader, from a first reading of the application, considered that a decision of intentional homelessness was possible.

'Settlement cases' involved the situation where the homeless applicant had lived abroad and had given up this accommodation prior to coming to Great Britain and applying for housing. Where, however, an applicant had given up accommodation in Great Britain prior to applying as a homeless person, the case would be categorised as a 'B' case—possibly intentionally homeless, but not on settlement grounds. A different internal categorisation was made despite the fact that legally they involved the same issues—whether Timbergreens was satisfied that the applicant became homeless intentionally. The manager explained why the distinction between 'A' (settlement) and 'B' (non-settlement) cases existed:

> It's complexity . . . [I]n this authority people who come from abroad pre-dominantly come from [southern Asia], often for the same reasons—there's a better lifestyle available over here than there was over there—and if you look at a 'B' case there's a million and one reasons why a case could fall into a 'B' category. It could be rent arrears, mortgage arrears, tied tenancies which are a nightmare, people who just abandon properties . . .
>
> (*Manager, Timbergreens*)

The typological distinction within PIH cases had considerable significance in terms of the way the decision-making process unfolded for particular types of cases. Different patterns of work flowed from different categorisation of cases. Indeed, settlement cases were allocated to less senior officers because they were regarded as being more straightforward.

The casework team had developed a procedures manual which contained specific guidance to caseworkers about how to carry out interviews for settlement cases. Similar guidance, however, was not introduced for non-settlement cases. The manager explained:

> If you can write a procedures guide then you should do so, so that people know what they're supposed to be doing and why they're supposed to be

doing it. It was done on settlement intentionals because they do follow a fairly similar format in the vast majority of cases. There are too many 'ifs' and 'buts' on things like rent arrears.

(Manager, Timbergreens)

Two-thirds of Timbergreen's judicial review experiences had involved intentional homelessness decisions. Most of these (50 per cent of its overall judicial review caseload) had involved 'settlement' cases. The content of the interview guidance had been developed (though not exclusively) in light of these experiences of judicial review. The number of questions which had to be asked of settlement applicants (as part of its 'information binge' already described) steadily increased with each judicial review:

Each [judicial review] that goes you find an increase in workload. You tend to have to ask more questions to cover the points that were raised in the judicial review where we were criticised, even though we probably won it. Where there's bits of criticism it's picked up on—'you've got to cover this angle, let's cover this angle.'

(Caseworker, Timbergreens)

The guidance comprised detailed instructions on the questions which had to be asked and the order in which they should be asked:

1. Why did the applicant go abroad?
2. How long did she/he expect to be away?
3. How did the applicant support him/herself and family?
4. Why did the applicant stay abroad for so long?
5. What were the full reasons for leaving the accommodation and returning to the UK?
6. Were there any reason why he/she and family could not continue to stay in the accommodation?
7. Did the applicant have any problems in the accommodation?
8. What arrangements were made for accommodation in the UK?

The above were the main questions which had been set down to be asked. However, many of these questions were accompanied by small explanatory notes and additional questions which should be asked. Accordingly, there were almost thirty standard questions which would be posed in the interview with settlement applicants.

Timbergreens, like the other housing authorities which took part in the research, operated under considerable pressure of time. The caseworkers felt extremely overworked. Nevertheless, they were aware of the need to obtain responses from settlement applicants for each question set out in the guidance. Despite the general pressure on their time, caseworkers would adhere strictly to the interview prompt, making such interviews laborious and long. It was not uncommon for them to take up to one and half hours to complete, or longer if an interpreter was being used. The desire to conclude the interview as quickly as possible and the need to demonstrate that all questions had received responses, however, imposed a formalism on the interview experience which lacked much of the flexibility and purposiveness of administrative law.

The example of case T44 illustrates the rigidity of the settlement interview and how it could impose a limit on the complexity of the applicant's account of their circumstances which was obtained from it. The applicant in T44 had previously lived in southern Asia and had relinquished accommodation there in order to come to the UK. On arrival in the UK she moved in with her husband and the husband's first wife. The applicant approached Timbergreens for assistance with housing when she was asked to leave the husband's home. The caseworker closely followed the procedure manual's guidance. The passage in the guidance which accompanied the question relating to what kind of arrangements an applicant made when leaving another country to come to the UK was as follows:

> The next question is of crucial significance to our reading of the applicant's case . . . [H]e/she should be asked *what arrangements were made for accommodation in the UK?* In order to check out the plausibility of the reply, the applicant should be encouraged to give full details of the arrangements— whether they were perceived to be temporary or permanent (reasons for forming these views) how they were affected etc. If no arrangements were made, or only temporary arrangements, ask the applicants what they expected upon their return to the UK. Also, be prepared to probe a little further and ask them to outline their longer term expectations (once again, reasons should be given for these expectations).

During the interview the following exchange took place between the caseworker and the applicant *via* Timbergreens' interpreter:

CASEWORKER ('CW'): What arrangements did she make for accommodation in the UK?

INTERPRETER ('INT'): She made no prior arrangements.

CW: What were her expectations in coming here?

INT: She hoped to live with her husband and his other wife.

CW: How long did she expect to stay in this arrangement?

INT: For as long as they would allow her.

CW: Did she perceive this as permanent or temporary?

INT: She thought it would be for a long time.

CW: Permanent then?

INT: Permanent.

CW: Did she check this out in advance?

INT: Yes, she contacted the husband and he said for her to come over.

CW: Did she discuss the details with her husband?

INT: No.

CW: Did she make any prior accommodation arrangements before coming to this country?

INT: Her husband phoned her and told her to come to the UK, but there was no discussion about how long she would be able to stay.

CW: How long did she think she would be able to live with her husband?

INT: She didn't know—she couldn't have had an idea about this.

It is clear that the caseworker faithfully adhered to the formal procedural guidance. She asked precisely the questions which appeared in the interview prompt. However, it can also be seen that it was necessary for her to get an answer which could be fitted into the possible pictures offered by the guidance. The applicant's answer to the question 'Did you perceive this as temporary or permanent?' was not satisfactory to the caseworker. Staying with her husband and husband's first wife for as long as they would allow, and hoping that this would be for a long time was not an adequate answer from the perspective of the caseworker. The applicant had to have perceived this arrangement as either permanent or temporary. The complexity of the relationship between the applicant, her husband and her husband's other family, and the messiness and lack of clarity surrounding the accommodation plans in the UK, required to be squeezed into the intelligible format of an 'either/or' dichotomy.

Timbergreens was legally conscientious about feeding its legal knowledge gained from judicial review into its casework routines. Its interview guide constitutes a good example of what Sossin (2004) describes as 'soft law', though of an informal kind. But the form this guidance took and the way it was used by caseworkers constituted a typically bureaucratic application of legal knowledge. Timbergreens responded to judicial review (in such cases) by developing detailed rules which could be followed routinely by bureaucrats. However, this approach lacks the flexibility of administrative law, and misses the purposiveness of administrative law's standards. The guidance proved to be rather constricting in the hands of certain caseworkers, and imposed a structure on the information that could be obtained from applicants. It defeated the administrative law principles of not fettering one's discretion, about giving the applicant the opportunity to present his/her case properly, and about openly and authentically considering all the relevant factors in an applicant's case.

The Spirit and Letter of Administrative Law

Another way of describing this tension between full compliance with administrative law and the bureaucratic mode of operation, is to frame it in terms of the letter and spirit of the law. The principles of administrative law, as general purposive standards, may be regarded as embodying the 'spirit' of administrative law. Particular judicial review decisions, on the other hand, where the principles have been applied to specific fact situations, constitute the 'letter' of administrative law. They are bounded, precise and particular manifestations of administrative law principles—administrative law in application. They are the equivalent of precise regulations. The argument here is that in responding to a precise ruling from a judicial review decision and consistently following it in future relevant cases, the government agency is being faithful to the letter of administrative law, but may miss the spirit.

The classic legal distinction between the letter and the spirit of the law, of course, has been adopted by McBarnet and Whelan (1991) to describe the practices of 'creative compliance'. Their argument, as already noted in the previous chapter, is that regulatees' *attitude* towards the goals of regulation prompts them to manipulate the letter of the law so as to violate its spirit. The argument being made here, however, is different and supplementary. It is that the regulatees' *legal competence* can also lead them to observe the letter of the law while violating its spirit. In other words, the spirit of the law may be defeated not just by a lack of legal conscientiousness, but by a lack of legal competence.

BOUNDED APPLICATION OF LEGAL KNOWLEDGE

The final point to be made in this chapter adds a third element to the notion of legal competence and describes another barrier to maximising compliance with administrative law. The section above noted that the bureaucratic mode of operation militates against the distillation of general administrative law principles from specific judicial review decisions. Such a process, of course, demands a certain amount of legal skill. Even if such a task were achieved—perhaps with the assistance of legal advisors or through legal training—there is a further requirement here in terms of maximising compliance with administrative law. After distilling a general principle from a specific judicial review decision, the decision-maker must then re-apply it to other relevant decision-making tasks within its remit. Compliance with administrative law requires the lawful exercise of discretion in all areas within an agency's remit.

The evidence from fieldwork, however, was that the housing authorities' responses to judicial review were much more localised to the specific area of decision-making which had been scrutinised in court. This suggests that the bureaucratic mode of operation may militate against the development of the legal skills involved in such a process. The thoughtful and skilled application of legal knowledge to other relevant areas of decision-making may in practice be overwhelmed by the pursuit of administrative efficiency or by fragmentation within a large organisation (see Daintith and Page, 1999: 314). We need look no further than the example of Timbergreens to illustrate this point. It is striking that the bulk of their efforts in responding conscientiously to judicial review was concentrated on enhancing interview guidance for settlement cases (which, as we have already noted above, formed a large part of their overall judicial review caseload). The application of legal knowledge, then, was bounded—restricted in the main to the 'type' of decision which had been judicially reviewed.

This kind of bounded response forms a barrier to full compliance with administrative law. The barrier is compounded, however, by the fact that there is a risk of complacency on the part of government agencies when they do make such limited responses. Lipsky has suggested that:

> By developing procedural rules agencies may in fact protect the rights of some clients, but they also gain legitimacy in continuing to act with most clients as they did before. (1980: 43)

There is a parallel, it is suggested, with administrative agencies' reactions to prolonged experiences of judicial review. It was striking during fieldwork that each of the local authorities expressed confidence in the 'rightness' of their decisions. Timbergreens and Eastbank, in particular, were particularly confident about their legal abilities. Indeed, their confidence extended to an inflated sense of their success rate in court. Eastbank's team leader (who had been solely involved in litigation by virtue of her role on the intentionality panel) estimated that Eastbank had successfully defended 90 per cent or 95 per cent of its judicial reviews. The statistics, however, present a more even picture, although one where Eastbank has been more successful than not. Up until the time of fieldwork Eastbank had successfully defended 67 per cent of its substantive judicial review hearings. Perceptions among Timbergreens' officers concerning the 'success rate' of its judicial review experience were that it had successfully defended most of them. The statistics, however, present a different picture. Timbergreens had successfully defended its substantive judicial review hearings in only 41 per cent of its cases. In relation to Muirfield, it was widely perceived within the casework team that it was 'extremely good' at judicial review and had successfully defended the vast majority of them. The statistics bear out the view that Muirfield had successfully defended most of its cases, although perhaps not quite to the extent which officers perceived. It had done so in 71 per cent of substantive judicial review hearings.

The irony here is that conscientiousness in the application of legal knowledge to decision-making routines can bring a self-confidence that may inhibit, rather than enhance, an overall compliance programme. It is a strange paradox that an increased exposure to judicial review can contribute to a reduction in the extent to which government agencies self-regulate their compliance with administrative law.

CONCLUSION

We explored the hypothesis in this chapter that judicial review's effectiveness in securing compliance with administrative law will be enhanced where decision-makers' legal competence is greater. By 'legal competence' I referred to the ability to interpret administrative law in the same terms as the courts, to distil general principles for wide application to specific situations, and to apply those principles to all relevant areas within the decision-maker's remit. However, we saw in this chapter that there is much that stands in the way of such legal competence.

The problem of legal competence parallels the issue of matching rule-type and enforcement strategy, the importance of which has been highlighted in the regulation literature. The choice of rule type may hinder or enhance regulatory effectiveness. Baldwin (1995) suggests that rule-makers should fashion rules to take into account the demands of different enforcement techniques. It is worth noting, however, that administrative law's enforcement technique (review initiated by complainant) is ill-matched to its rule type (general purposive standards). Black (1997), on the other hand, has shown that general purposive rules require a corresponding interpretive community to maximise effectiveness. Shared understandings between regulator and regulatee are required so that the general rules are applied appropriately in accordance with the purpose of the rule. A quick consideration of administrative law and judicial review, however, shows that there is a deficiency here also. The *ad hoc* nature of administrative law 'enforcement' through judicial review litigation, and the formal and clinically removed nature of the Administrative Court as a forum for enforcement, are inimical to the development of an interpretive community. Yet, the absence of an interpretive community between the courts and the administration in the face of the general and imprecise quality of administrative law principles would seem to contribute to administrative law's ineffectiveness in terms of its ability to control government.

This chapter concludes our direct discussion of the decision-makers and the hypotheses which relate to them. A focus on the decision-makers in isolation, however, would provide too atomistic an analysis of government administration. Decision-making takes place within an environment which structures and informs the exercise of government discretion. The decision-making environment, accordingly, constitutes the focus of the next chapter and the third part of this book, and it is to this that we now turn.

Part 3: The Decision-Making Environment

5

The Decision-Making Environment

INTRODUCTION

H AVING EXPLORED IN the previous chapters the first element of the
administrative realm, the decision-makers, this chapter considers
the second element—the environment in which administrative decisions are made. An exploration of the decision-making environment is
important because it situates individual decision-making practices
within broader contexts that influence, inform and structure the use of
discretion on the ground. A focus on the decision-making environment,
therefore, makes a link between the micro and the macro and attempts
to trace the relationships between individual legal decisions and
broader society.

The main point here—quite a simple one—is that government
agencies do not operate in a social, political or economic vacuum. Law
is not the only normative system within the decision-making environment. There is a relationship—which is not so simple—between decision-making inside an organisation and social forces outside it. One of
the main tasks of organisational sociology is to try and understand this
relationship (or, more accurately, these relationships), and one of the
main tasks of socio-legal studies of administrative decision-making is
to understand the particular significance of law.

The decision-making environment, then, can be characterised as a
space where law and alternative normative influences co-exist. The
extent of the competition between law and other normative systems
(where one exists) will vary according to context, and within the same
context across time. The hypothesis which relates to the decision-
making environment is that judicial review's effectiveness in securing
compliance with administrative law will be enhanced where the
competition between law and other normative forces is non-existent,
or, if a competition exists, where law's strength is increased in the
environment. This hypothesis draws attention to the fact that the

decision-making environment, in both direct and indirect, obvious and subtle ways, is capable of pulling decision-makers in a number of directions.

The aim of this chapter is to demonstrate the significance of this condition by using homelessness administration to illustrate how competing forces may co-exist within the administrative arena. The examples given here, then, emerged from fieldwork and, as such, are not intended to comprise a complete list of the environmental pressures on government decision-making. Such is considerably beyond the scope of this study. They are meant to be merely illustrative, rather than exhaustive.

THE PLURALITY OF NORMATIVE SYSTEMS WITHIN THE DECISION-MAKING ENVIRONMENT

Law is certainly a normative system within the decision-making environment, but it is only one of them. Other direct accountability pressures exist alongside legality. Colin Scott (2000) has drawn our attention to the plurality of accountability regimes which are imposed on government agencies and argues for a model of 'extended account-ability' which reflects the dense network of accountability mechanisms which now exist. For example, Hood et al (1999) describe the history of local government regulation, noting a striking overall growth over the last 25 years or so. Local government is now subject to a rather frag-mented system of oversight which is the product of piecemeal reform (1999: 114). Local government, as a 'regulatory space' (Hancher and Moran, 1989), has become increasingly crowded with various regula-tors and formal accountability regimes. In addition to administrative law and the courts, a number of other systems exist. The Audit Commission oversees the Best Value regime under the Local Government Act 1999, designed to achieve best value in the perfor-mance of local government duties according the three 'E's'—effective-ness, economy and efficiency (Vincent-Jones, 2000). The Commission for Local Administration provides local government ombudsmen under the Local Government Act 1974, empowered to investigate complaints of injustice arising out of maladministration and to provide guidance to promote fair and effective administration (Seneviratne, 2002: chapter 6). Additionally, there are sector specific specialised inspectorates (Hood et al, 1999: chapter 5), and more informal regulatory influences such as, in relation to housing, the Good Practice Unit of the Chartered Institute of Housing. Lastly, there are internal complaints systems which were a feature of the Citizen's Charter (Page, 1999) and now the Service First programme. It remains substantially unclear how these regimes mingle and compete within the administrative arena and we have much still to learn about the complex relationships between the various accountability regimes and mundane administrative decision-making on the ground.

In this section we look at our case study of homelessness decision-making to identify alternative normative influences within the decision-making environment which, as we shall see, competed with law for normative supremacy.

Financial Management

The first accountability pressure which is described here and which competed with law within the decision-making environment concerns financial management.

Case Study of Eastbank and Temporary Accommodation Pressures

The pressure of managing limited finances and being accountable for budget expenditures had a clear influence on decision-making practices. We have noted already in chapter 3, in relation to Timbergreens, that the HPU manager's budgetary constraints led him to engage in the creative avoidance of temporary accommodation duties. Similar (perhaps more acute) pressures were felt in Eastbank. Eastbank Council as a whole operated on a business unit basis. The HPU was 'contracted' by an internal 'client' and was accountable to the client for its expenditure, performance and value for money. An evident and major concern of the HPU during fieldwork related to a significant overspend in relation to its temporary accommodation budget. At the time of fieldwork, the HPU was projected to overspend by approximately £640,000 which represented (approximately) a 10 per cent overspend for the year. There were fears of job losses as a result of the financial predicament and rumours were rife among officers about what might happen by the end of the financial year. The overspend was symptomatic of the high level of demand and a general shortage of temporary accommodation units. On a day-to-day basis, the most pressing difficulty was the lack of B&Bs to temporarily house the constant flow of applicants who required them. In the years prior to fieldwork, due to an upturn in the housing market, the numbers of private landlords who were willing to lease their properties to Eastbank for use as temporary accommodation diminished. This exacerbated the pressure on B&B usage—the most expensive form of temporary accommodation. A recent regeneration programme also had an impact on the demand for temporary accommodation. A previously run-down area with poor housing stock had been used as a way of getting people out of B&B accommodation. Permanent housing offers in the poor accommodation were made in the confidence that most applicants would refuse and so could then be 'discharged' from temporary accommodation. After the regeneration programme this option was no longer available:

> A lot of people have never sat back and realised what Eastbank did in the last two or three years . . . We're knocking down [estate A]. [Estate A] was a sort of discharge. Let's say you have four voids in [estate A]. Out of those four voids, if you offer it to four families, three of them are going to say 'No', so you discharge. For about two years now we haven't had that. And when you can discharge at least three or four people every week, that's 20 families you can kick out of B&B straight away or whatever . . . But I don't know if members or the people upstairs were aware of the fact that these were the major places that we discharged people into. We'd say 'you've got to go there. There's nothing wrong with it.' And some people would take it and some people would not. But if you haven't got those avenues it means in a way that your [temporary accommodation] will increase, because what you have to give people is off-estate properties and properties that are going to be nicer than before.
>
> (*Manager, Eastbank*)

Policy Initiatives to Reduce Expenditure

Temporary accommodation expenditure, therefore, was a major strategic problem for Eastbank to overcome. Eastbank's senior manager, who was responsible for devising strategy, was conscious of his predicament and the implications for policy development:

> On average our acceptance rate I think is now something like 31 per cent. That's good, but there's pain somewhere else. There's pain in the voluntary sector, 'coz people that we used to accept are not being accepted any more. So someone else is having to pick up the can, the burden. Someone else is spreading the money . . . We're just about to put forward projections now for next year about what we want to spend on temporary accommodation. What I believe is going to happen is they'll say again 'We want to cut it by

half a million' and I'll have to go back to the drawing board and say 'How can I further stop homeless households being accepted into [Eastbank]?' And that's unfortunately the game we're in. . . I'm trying to put forward policies that are going to stop people coming to the door and still keep in touch with my human side. Have I done that? I don't know. That's for someone else to judge.

(*Senior manager, Eastbank*)

The senior manager, as indicated above, had made a number of policy changes to try and reduce temporary accommodation expenditure. The criteria used to determine priority need received particular attention. First, the age limit for the automatic granting of priority need status was raised from 60 years to 65 years. Secondly, the threshold for awarding priority need for medical problems was also raised. When an applicant had medical problems, the medical advisor rated the severity of the problems on a scale of points. Previously, if the applicant received a rating of 15 points or more they would be deemed to be in priority need. This threshold was raised to 20 points as a result of the temporary accommodation crisis. Further, the medical advisors were instructed not to regard alcoholism or drug use as grounds for priority need. The final change related to young people leaving care or institutions. Previously, such persons of up to the age of 21 years were automatically accorded priority need status. This age bar was removed, so that no applicants in this situation would automatically be deemed to be in priority need.

Casework Practices to Reduce Expenditure

In addition to these clear internal policy shifts, individual caseworkers also modified their decision-making practices in light of the emerging culture of financial stringency. One caseworker noted:

The mood has changed. We're all very reluctant to put people in B&B, especially if you've been told if the costs of B&B go up further—you know, you get snide remarks that you'll be out the door . . . The practice now is prevention of B&B at all costs.

(*Caseworker, Eastbank*)

Caseworkers had developed a number of techniques at avoiding B&B placements and were quite skilled at it.

The usual aim was to persuade applicants to find their own temporary accommodation, or where this was not possible, to postpone for as long as possible the moment when B&B would have to be given.

Cases E92 and E93 provide examples. E92 was dealt with over the reception desk. The applicant had an appointment booked for a few weeks hence to discuss her application in detail, but had prematurely been told to leave her temporary accommodation. Accordingly, she required temporary accommodation pending a determination of her application. The applicant had a child. She had claimed Child Benefit for the child, but her claim had not yet been processed. The caseworker told the applicant that she could not be placed into B&B until she was in receipt of Child Benefit. B&B was accordingly refused and the applicant was told to return when her claim was processed. 'That's one gone' the caseworker said to me as we moved on to case E93. There was no legal basis to the caseworker's claim. Instead, receipt of Child Benefit was a common method used by Eastbank to 'confirm' a mother's priority need status—that there was a dependent child. Nevertheless, this technique was successful in postponing the use of B&B.

The applicant in E93 was a former tenant of Eastbank. She was a student and so not entitled to Housing Benefit. On the way to see this applicant, the caseworker calculated out loud the possible cost to the applicant if she insisted in being offered B&B: 'let's say £20 per day to put her off—that's £140 per week.' She too, then, had to find alternative temporary accommodation.

In other instances, however, Eastbank solved the problem on the ground by getting rid of the applicant. Particular 'types' of applicants could trigger this response, some of which were based on ethnic stereotyping (Halliday, 2000b). For example, in case E38, the customers were a family of Irish travellers—a married couple with six children, the youngest of which was three weeks old. They claimed that they had been living in an unofficial travellers' site in Ireland but had to leave there when they experienced harassment from the wife's family. They sold their caravan and came over to England as the husband had previously lived there. It was not possible to gain confirmation of the story from any external sources. The caseworker asked the team leader for advice. It transpired that another family of Irish travellers had also approached Eastbank on the same day. The team leader presumed they had come over together. The team leader himself had asked for the advice of the manager who decided that they should not be offered any assistance. The team leader explained that there once was a time when such families would have been placed in temporary accommodation pending enquiries, but that 'with the squeeze' (meaning the financial restrictions) no assistance would be given, adding, 'it would open the floodgates'. The caseworker asked what reason for refusing assistance should be stated in the decision letter. Just at that point, the manager walked past and the team leader explained that a further family of travellers had applied for housing. The manager asked the caseworker if she had asked for a receipt of sale of the caravan. She explained that it hadn't occurred to her to do so. 'It doesn't matter', replied the manager, 'we can't house them anyway'. He explained that it was getting into 'silly season' when 'all sorts' would be coming over and applying for help.

After the manager left, the team leader acknowledged that Eastbank was doing something 'dodgy' with this case. He told the caseworker to write in the decision letter that Eastbank was not satisfied that the family had made enough of their own efforts to find accommodation. The manager had suggested that the decision-letter should state that Eastbank was not satisfied as to the truth of the family's claim about being homeless. The reasoning to be given in the decision-letter did not seem to be important.

Conclusion

Loveland (1995) has demonstrated the relationship between housing resources and the content of homelessness decisions. His thesis is that diminishing long-term housing resources leads to restrictive decision-making. The case study of Eastbank shows that a shortage of temporary accommodation problems can have the same effect. Financial stringency is a very strong influence within the decision-making environment, and one, as the example from Eastbank shows, that can trickle down to individual decision-making on the ground, as well as resulting in more obvious policy shifts. This is not to suggest, of course, that financial pressures are always in competition with legal requirements. There are certainly situations where the two sets of demands may coincide or where the agency may make financial savings within a lawful margin of discretion. But often this is not the case. In both Timbergreens and Eastbank, there was considerable evidence—particularly in relation to the fulfilment of temporary accommodation duties—of unlawful decision-making as a direct result of financial pressures.

Performance Audit

Michael Power (1997) has charted and assessed the rise of auditing mechanisms in society. Government has not escaped these developments. The increased significance of audit to government has been the subject of sustained analysis and critique (see Cowan and Halliday, 2003: 88–92). The 'Best Value' regime provides, perhaps, the most stark example of performance auditing in local government. Best Value replaced the system of Compulsory Competitive Tendering and has been described as marking a change in regulatory style—a move away from coercion to 'responsibilisation' (Vincent-Jones, 2002). It is certainly clear that such systems of performance audit exert a strong influence on individual decision-making practices on the ground. Cowan and Halliday (2003), for example, describe the significance of the Best Value regime to local government decision-making in their study of internal review and homelessness administration. They note in relation to one of their case studies (2003: chapter 4) how a discourse of efficiency, informed by the Best Value regime, is capable of overwhelming concerns with legality.

Case Study of Muirfield and Performance Related Pay

Fieldwork for this project took place before the introduction of the Best Value regime. Nevertheless, some of the local authorities had introduced internal systems of performance audit which had a similarly strong influence on decision-making. Muirfield, for example, had introduced a system of performance related pay. Performance was assessed according to certain performance indicators which are not dissimilar from those of the Best Value regime. Caseworkers were given a number of targets. For example, the number of active cases was to be maintained within a limit of 30. Further, cases were to be decided within 18 working days. Periodically, caseworkers were assessed according to their performance and graded on a scale of 1 to 6. Corresponding financial bonuses were awarded.

The HPU's manager regarded the scheme as having been successful, in that targets in general had been met, and that officers had been 'switched on' to it. However, some caseworkers felt very aggrieved about this method of assessing their performance. They noted that the assessment was driven by a purely statistical exercise and took no account of the less quantifiable aspects of the quality of decision-making, echoing Power's critique of the audit society:

> The audit society is a society that endangers itself because it invests too heavily in shallow rituals of verification at the expense of other forms of organisational intelligence. (1997: 123)

Further, however, caseworkers expressed the view that the method of assessment not only ignored more meaningful quality indicators, but actively encouraged poor decision-making, in that officers were rewarded for resolving cases quickly. Rather than taking an extra amount of time to conduct further enquiries which may shed light on a case, some officers, it was suggested, made 'daft' decisions in order to keep their statistics down, not caring about the impact of their decisions on the plight of the applicants. One officer indicated that he was aware of colleagues having 'binned' such daft decisions so that they could not be examined by an auditor. In general, caseworkers recognised a competition between the meeting of targets and the depth of casework:

> CASEWORKER: Because you try to meet an 18 day target, then a lot of times you're rushing things and you may cut off an enquiry, or not go the whole route because it's going to take you extra time. I think we all cut corners to get round a decision or sometimes you make a wrong decision because you can't spend any time looking at it any further. And also because Muirfield interprets things so strictly, you don't allow enough flexibility for people where you should be more flexible. You can't just say, just because someone doesn't fit the exact criteria that this is the result, coz there are reasons why people don't in certain ways, coz they're people—they make mistakes. I don't think we allow enough for mistakes.
> INTERVIEWER: Do you think cutting corners inclines itself to a particular case outcome?
> CASEWORKER: We're more inclined to reject.

Team leaders were also subject to performance targets. Their assessments, of course, corresponded to how well their caseworkers performed. The influence on caseworker decision-making of performance audit, then, was also experienced through the pressure from team leaders:

> I'm not saying targets in themselves are bad. Targets in themselves are good . . . but the targets to [the team leaders] are life and death . . . They will go on and on and on and on about those targets . . . Because of that, there are certain sacrifices and certain compromises that you do make. I'm not saying

that everyone is sold out to the targets, but most of us are on performance related pay, and performance related pay is linked to those targets. Therefore, there are compromises made in that way, and I think that that has weakened the quality and the depth of the casework . . .

(*Caseworker, Muirfield*)

Conclusion

Performance audit and its focus on efficiency sits in some tension with legality. As we shall see in Part 4 of this book, administrative law is sufficiently flexible to retain competing images of administrative justice, one of which promotes the value of efficiency. However, administrative law does not project this image of administrative justice into all decision-making contexts, and even when it does, it does not promote efficiency at all costs. Some (perhaps many) of the compromises in casework mentioned above would be regarded as unlawful. The fact that caseworkers actively hide some decisions from future inspection lends weight to this view. Further, the caseworkers' own discomfort at the pressure they feel and the decisions they make in light of it testify to these problematic practices. Performance audit inclines towards quantifiable calculus to the neglect of more elusive criteria. The legality of administrative decision-making, however, inclines towards such elusive or 'softer' criteria. There is an inevitable degree of tension, then, between performance audit in its current guise and legality. The degree of tension will, of course, vary according to context. But some degree of tension, it is suggested, will exist as the above examples of fieldwork suggest.

Political Pressure

Government, of course, operates within an intimate political context. Administrative decision-makers are accountable to their political masters. Political pressure, direct and indirect, is another important force within the decision-making environment. Indeed, Daintith and Page note the significance of political context to the nature of legal advice to central government departments (1999: 325–26). In this section, however, we consider the impact of a local political context to administrative decision-making in Muirfield.

Case Study of Muirfield and Local Political Antipathy Towards the Homeless

Of the three field sites, Muirfield operated within the political context which gave the clearest directives to the bureaucracy about homelessness administration. It took a particularly harsh line in relation to homelessness decision-making. Such an approach was encouraged and enabled by the political climate of the council. It was widely perceived among officers at all levels of the HPU that Muirfield's councillors actively desired the minimisation of council assistance to homeless people:

> Homelessness is seen as the carbuncle on the bum of Muirfield, a burden … The overriding factor is that the politicians want us to be as tough as possible. They want us to deter as many people as possible from coming to Muirfield. That's an actual quote from a councillor
>
> *(Caseworker, Muirfield)*

The manager, too, was aware of this restrictive political climate. He observed that councillors were pleased when Muirfield received bad publicity regarding its homelessness functions as it might act as a deterrent against future applications. Like the caseworker above, the manager noted a lack of priority accorded to the homeless population by Muirfield's councillors:

> Councillors are not interested in homelessness. They're not interested in homeless people. There are very few councillors' enquiries [on homelessness] when you compare them with other councillors' enquiries that we get. The main reason for that is because the majority of people we place as homeless are not placed in Muirfield, so they don't have easy access to their councillor and they're not a voter either. The people with a voice in Muirfield are the tenants.
>
> *(Manager, Muirfield)*

Muirfield's robust line was further evidenced, as we saw in chapter 3, by its limitless budget to defend judicial review litigation and its policy of doing so on every occasion. Some of the caseworkers were uncomfortable with this approach and engaged in what I have described as 'subversive' decision-making (Halliday, 2000a) where they would try and manipulate the decision-making process at various stages in order to achieve converse aims. We saw in chapter 2 that the decision-making process is sufficiently fragmented that individual officers retain the discretion to try and steer decisions down a chosen course. Indeed, such fragmentation in the decision-making process is what has led a number of researchers to focus on intra-organisation dynamics in stressing, conversely, the limits of judicial review's impact (see Bridges, Game, Lomas, 1987; Sunkin and Le Sueur, 1991; Mullen, Pick and Prosser, 1996). Muirfield's drafting of the case recommendation for consideration by the team leader provided one such opportunity to engage in subversive decision-making. However, caseworkers were aware that often their efforts were thwarted. Indeed, there were many aspects of the bureaucratic system which were stacked against them. For example, we have already noted that the computerised system which recorded information about applications and stored decision-letter templates did not permit caseworkers to write acceptance letters without a team leader's authorisation, though it did permit caseworkers to write refusal letters under their own authority. Such features of the bureaucratic infrastructure reveal organisational priorities.

The local political environment of antipathy towards the homeless, however, was also felt more directly in terms of the supervision of caseworkers by their team leaders. One caseworker described how his conscientious approach to drafting decision-letters was overruled by a team leader:

CASEWORKER: What I originally did was, at each point, I would put down case law to substantiate why I had made that decision. Especially in terms of intentionality, I'd show him how I'd been objective for both sides and I'd put relevant case law. And I was told there was too much bullshit in it. I was told to cut out the bullshit and the bit he said was bullshit was the case law—'Don't put the case law in'.
INTERVIEWER: What did he mean by that?
CASEWORKER: He's saying that if I put in case law I'm laying open my work and my thoughts on how I reached the decision. Subsequently, it is easier for opposing counsel to take that apart, and show where I had gone wrong. But I said, 'Surely, the principle is that if I am reaching a decision that we've haven't got a duty to these people, if I've made a wrong decision, surely I should be saying this is where you've gone wrong, this is what you should have done.' I thought that was only fair and right. [The team leader] said., 'No, you're not in this business to be fair and equal to clients, your job is just to,' (what was it he said?) basically to fuck them off—that was the jist of it. So I don't put in any case law any more.

Conclusion

Political influence over administrative decision-making can be overt and extreme, as the 'homes for votes' saga in the London Borough of Westminster demonstrated (see Cowan, 2003). However, in a less sensational and more routine fashion, administrative decision-makers are conscious of working within an immediate political environment and are aware of local political initiatives and proclivities. Cowan and Halliday (2003: chapter 3) demonstrated how a local political concern over antisocial behaviour impacted on homelessness decision-making practices in one of their case studies, provoking a discourse of risk over the tenantability of housing applicants. Similarly in Muirfield, the local political apathy towards homelessness applicants created the conditions for harsh policies and restrictive individual decision-making by street-level officers. It must be stressed, of course, that, just like the other accountability pressures, political pressures are not always in competition with the concerns of legality. But it is clear that they are at times, and can operate to overwhelm the normative force of law within the decision-making environment.

More Remote Social/Political Features

In addition to formal accountability regimes there are more remote features of the political, social and economic landscape which nevertheless inform decision-making. In relation to homelessness administration, for example, broad political currents around contentious issues such as social welfare provision, housing, immigration, and so forth, form part of the background landscape against which individual decision-making takes place. Cowan and Halliday (2003: 129–30) have shown how these more remote features of the social and political landscape can inform housing applicants' perceptions of the bureaucratic process and their faith in the welfare system, which can in turn influence their decisions about whether or not to challenge adverse decisions. A parallel dynamic between features of the background landscape and individual decision-making is applicable to the bureaucrats themselves as we shall see further below.

Keith Hawkins (2002: 48) uses the concept of 'the surround' to assist in the understanding of legal decision-making. The surround, one of three organising concepts (along with 'the field' and 'the frame') directs our attention to the very broad, less direct environment in which decision-making takes place. In the context of health and safety regulation, he uses the example of unexpected disasters, such as the explosion and fire at the Piper Alpha oil rig, which can raise public and political fears or consciousness about public safety. Such events can alter the landscape which forms the background to the decision-making enterprise. Changes in the surround, Hawkins suggests, may influence decision-making on the ground either through central policy shifts which filter through to the front-line workers (a change in the field), or through front-line workers modifying their interpretive behaviour in light of the developing surround (a change in the frame).

Lipsky has similarly suggested that broad cultural values will inform street-level bureaucratic decision-making:

> Prevailing attitudes toward the poor permit rationalization of patterns that result in client neglect, which would be more difficult to rationalize if clients were middle class and generally respected . . . Intersecting with attitudes toward the stigmatised poor are attitudes prevalent in the larger society regarding clients' racial or ethnic backgrounds. Racism also affects the extent to which public employees regard clients as worthy, and it affects the extent to which patterns of practice evolve that distinguish among clients in terms of their racial backgrounds. (1980: 182)

The case study of Eastbank may well constitute an example of a such a dynamic in action. In chapter 3 we noted how a culture of suspicion could crystallise in relation to particular 'types' of applicant. We observed that immigrants constituted one of the types of applicant who were vulnerable to suspicion about dishonesty and abuse of the system. We also noted earlier in this chapter that Irish travellers constituted another 'type' of suspect applicant in Eastbank. Fieldwork in Eastbank took place following legislative changes to homelessness law which restricted the rights of homelessness applicants. Cowan (1997) has presented an analysis of these legislative changes and argues persuasively that they constituted a governmental response to the problem of a deficit of low-cost housing for public consumption. This understanding of the problem as a crisis of resources, however, was obscured by media constructions of 'the homeless problem' which focused on the 'bogus' claims of certain applicants—notably single mothers, travellers and immigrants. Decision-making at a local level in Eastbank, then, took place against a backdrop of increasing governmental restraint in terms of housing provision, and public apathy towards the plight of the homeless, fuelled by individualistic media constructions of the homeless problem.

The data collected in fieldwork, unfortunately, is not well-equipped to assess the extent to which the broad context of the legislative changes informed Eastbank's suspicion about Irish Travellers or immigrants. Such connections, certainly in relation to this data set, are very much suggested, though they did not emerge overtly from the data. At one level, of course, such connections must always be a matter of faith. The more subtle the influence of the background features, the more one has to rely on proposing the explanation, rather than on discovering it from 'harder' data such as exists in relation to more direct accountability pressures.

Of course, there is also a sense in which the distinction between direct accountability pressures and the more remote features of the social and political environment is an artificial one. The rise of performance audit and the financial pressures within which local government operates are, for example, a reflection of shifting political and public consciousness about what matters in public administration—the widespread shift towards 'New Public Management' (Hood, 1990). Similarly, local political pressures may reflect broader political currents. The point here is that there is a dynamic between the background landscape, more direct accountability pressures, and individual decision-making practices. The separation of these contexts for analytical purposes is not intended to obscure the fluid dynamic between them or the complexity of their inter-relationships. Rather, the aim is to paint a reasonably broad and complex picture of the decision-making environment where remote features can nevertheless create the conditions for more localised shifts in policy and legislation and, at times, penetrate administrative culture more directly and act in competition with legality as an informant of decision-making.

WHAT CONDITIONS LAW'S STRENGTH IN THE ENVIRONMENT?

So far this chapter has made the point that the decision-making environment is an arena where law is but one of a number of normative forces. Judicial review's capacity to secure compliance with administrative law will be enhanced where law is not in competition with the alternative influences—where there is a convergence of normative systems (Kagan et al, 2003). However, the case study of homelessness administration demonstrated that law *was* in competition with the other forces in that context. And it is suggested that this is perhaps the norm rather than the exception. Judicial review's capacity to secure compliance with administrative law, correspondingly, will be enhanced when the power of law is strengthened within the decision-making environment. This leads us to the question of what conditions law's strength when competing with other influences in the environment.

Unfortunately, this is by no means a straightforward question to answer. It is, of course, a matter for empirical enquiry. The strength of law in the decision-making environment can be determined only through an investigation of administrative agencies' responses to their environment. Intimate ethnographic descriptions of mundane administration will reveal that bureaucracies are quite chaotic enterprises where decision-makers display quite schizophrenic qualities. Administrative agencies as organisations have quite complex characters and display conflicting characteristics. Like humans (and because in part they are staffed by humans) they can be two-faced, or, more accurately, multifaced. The social reality is that the different normative systems which inhabit the decision-making environment are constantly being internalised by decision-makers to different extents and at different times. The competition between law and other normative forces is repeatedly played out across many sites within the decision-making process, producing quite a complicated and fragmented picture of the range of administrative values and their relative importance. This makes our understanding of the particular significance of the decision-making environment quite difficult. Further ethnographic work spanning the full range of levels within an administrative organisation is required to explore these micro-mezzo-macro links. The data from this study is, unfortunately, not well equipped to this task. Fieldwork, as indicated in chapter 1, was largely contained to front-line decision-making teams. A broader and more comprehensive approach is needed for a fuller understanding of the relationships between environmental normative pressures and internal decision-making. Ethnographic studies of front-line decision-making can demonstrate that competing discourses exist on the ground and that different accountability regimes influence decision-making at different times, but a broader multi-level perspective is required to understand why different normative systems are dominant at different times. Such, of course, as already suggested, is not an easy task.

Nevertheless, some general comments can be made here which, while resisting the temptation to be too definitive, may at least help to orient future enquiry. Some basic insights from the regulation literature about the features of law which condition its strength in the environment may be offered. Three features are focused on here. First, we examine the extent to which judicial review operates as a sanction; secondly, we explore the role of negotiation and persuasion in enforcement; and thirdly, we explore the flexibility of law in alternating between sanctioning and persuading enforcement strategies.

The Role of Sanctions

The more judicial review operates as a sanction against decision-makers, the greater will law's strength be in the decision-making environment, though its relative strength will depend on a comparison with the sanctioning power of competing normative forces.

Of course, it is fairly obvious that the extent to which judicial review may operate as a sanction against decision-makers is quite limited. The court may grant an order of *mandamus*, requiring the respondent body to perform a specific duty, but more often the court will grant an order of *certiorari* quashing an unlawful decision and requiring it, therefore, to be made again. In either case, however, the element of sanction in any formal sense is pretty minimal.

More informally, fieldwork demonstrated that the experience of being criticised in court could act as a kind of sanction. It can damage the professional pride of a decision-maker. For example, in Muirfield, one caseworker noted:

> When I was sat in the court and the judge [criticised my decision-letter], although he wasn't saying it to me personally, I went as red as a beetroot. He couldn't miss who it was he was talking about. I was sitting there beaming. And I thought 'Oh no, beam me up Scottie.' I didn't like that at all. So, subsequently, I got my shit together. That gave me personally the spur not to go there again.
>
> (*Caseworker, Muirfield*)

Such a finding is consistent with previous research which noted a sense of crisis consequent to initial experiences of litigation (Bridges et al, 1987; Sunkin and Le Sueur, 1991; Buck, 1998). However, this discomfort at judicial censure can wane with experience, illustrating the importance of exploring judicial review's impact across time (Sunkin and Pick, 2001). It certainly seemed to wane in Muirfield. From the perspective of Muirfield's manager and team leaders, litigation was an inevitable part of the job which did not reflect on their professional competence. One of the team leaders noted, 'I never think "Oh God, I lost that case." I don't think along those lines . . .' Rather, it was an aspect of their duties which they enjoyed, regardless of the outcome.

Additionally, of course, the financial costs of litigation, particularly if one loses and has to bear the costs of the other party, can operate as a sanction. Once again, however, the case study of Muirfield shows that the internal financial procedures of government agencies can preclude financial considerations falling within the remit of the decision-makers being litigated. Legal costs may come out of another department's budget.

In short, particularly in relation to other forms of regulation, judicial review is rather limited in the extent to which it may operate as a sanction. However, it should be noted that the extent to which judicial review will operate as a sanction may vary according to context. As we noted in chapter 1, homelessness administration is an example of what Galligan has described as 'individualised, adjudicative decisions' (1986: 237). In such contexts where individual decision are being made constantly on a grand scale, judicial review has a particularly restricted capacity to act as a sanction against decision-makers. The incidence of judicial review must inevitably be sporadic relative to the volume of decisions being processed, and in this sense the stakes are very low in relation to the threat posed by judicial review. This situation is compounded by the fact that the take-up of rights of redress is generally quite low. Genn (1999) has demonstrated that, in general, the pursuit of grievances through legal action is reasonably rare. Her study in England and Wales showed that only 14 per cent of non-trivial justiciable problems were resolved through adjudication (1999: 150). The figure was even smaller in Scotland at 9 per cent (Genn and Paterson, 2001: 158). Genn's survey was general in scope but did not cover grievances against government decision-making in any depth. The proportion of justiciable problems within Genn's sample dealing with claims against government bodies was very small. Comparable research in relation to administrative grievances remains to be conducted. Nevertheless, her research demonstrates clearly that, in general, the adjudication of problems is by far an exceptional outcome. There is no reason to suspect that the situation in relation to grievances against mass decision-making by government agencies is any different. Indeed, it is probably lower. Research in the field of social welfare repeatedly demonstrates the take up of rights of redress is extremely low (Sainsbury and Eardley, 1991; Dalley and Berthoud, 1992; Genn, 1994; Cowan and Halliday, 2003).

In other decision-making contexts, however, where decision-making is more prolonged, less routinised and decisions are fewer in number, the stakes may be correspondingly higher and judicial review may pose more of a threat and operate more as a sanction. This may, in part, account for the overwhelming success of judicial review in transforming the rule-making process in the United States. The cost to regulatory agencies of losing in court may provoke considerable caution in decision-making. Of course, there may be other reasons why the stakes are high in relation to judicial review litigation. There may be significant political fall-out from high level ministerial decisions which are challenged in court, bringing negative publicity and possible defeat (see Sunkin, 2004).

There is some scope, in short, for the sanctioning power of judicial review to vary according to context. Where it is greater, so will judicial review's power be within the decision-making environment.

Persuasion

However, as much of the regulation literature has demonstrated, sanctioning is not the only way to influence administrative decision-making. Law's power within the decision-making environment may be strengthened through processes of persuasion whereby legal conscientiousness may correspondingly be enhanced through dialogue. Research has consistently demonstrated that co-operative approaches to regulation have a greater capacity to develop shared sensibilities between regulator and regulatee (see, for example, Bardach and Kagan, 1982; Black, 1998; Hertogh, 2001; Braithwaite, 2002). In this sense, the power of law may be strengthened in the environment where opportunities are provided to persuade the regulatee of the virtue of its values and requirements.

Of course, once again, it is fairly obvious that judicial review is lacking in this regard. There is, under its current guise, no real capacity for persuasion or dialogue in judicial review litigation. Although this is a feature of law which conditions its strength within the environment, judicial review—certainly in its current form—is weak in this respect.

Flexibility

As the above two sub-sections have foreshadowed, a great deal of work on regulation has focused on the contrast between deterrence approaches to regulatory enforcement, where sanctions are used to encourage compliance, or co-operative approaches where compliance is achieved through negotiation and persuasion. The merits of these contrasting approaches has been the subject of some robust debate (Hawkins, 1990; Pearce and Tombs, 1990). However, as Braithwaite (1985) has noted (see also Kagan and Scholz, 1984), in terms of effectiveness, the important question is not whether to punish or persuade, but when to punish and when to persuade.[1] Indeed, the theory of responsive regulation (Ayres and Braithwaite, 1992) is premised on a flexible enforcement strategy which will permit a regulator to switch between punishment and persuasion in various degrees according to the behaviour, competence and attitude of the regulatee. A brief consideration of judicial review in such terms, of course, quickly reveals that it cannot be regarded as retaining any degree of flexibility. This is another feature of law which may render it weak within the decision-making environment when compared with some of the other normative influences.

CONCLUSION

Richardson and Machin (2000) in their study of the impact of judicial review on the workings of the Mental Health Review Tribunal have drawn our attention to the competition between strong value systems which can co-exist within the decision-making environment. The competition which they observed between a medical and legal system of knowledge represents, perhaps, an extreme case of the more common conflict of values which characterises the administrative arena. Different and, at times, competitive normative systems operate within the decision-making environment, and so law often has to compete for the normative attention of the decision-makers.

At this point we can see the link between our exploration of the decision-making environment in this chapter and our discussion of

---

[1] See Yeung (2004) however, for a normative critique on responsive regulation's focus on effectiveness.

legal conscientiousness in chapter 3. The decision-making environment offers the decision-maker a range of normative models of how the routine business of decision-making should unfold, and so makes various demands on the decision-maker. In chapter 3, I argued that one of the conditions for the maximisation of judicial review's effectiveness in securing compliance with administrative law was decision-makers' commitment to legality, whereby they care about lawfulness and so choose law above other normative forces. However, if the analysis stopped at this point it would be incomplete. We would be left with a very atomistic understanding of administrative decision-making. The purpose of this part of the book has been to supplement and develop the earlier analysis by recognising that decision-making behaviour is, to an extent, the product of its wider environment. The 'choice' of law above other normative forces is itself a social process which is conditioned by the dynamics of the decision-making environment. In other words, the conditions must be right for legal conscientiousness to be allowed to flourish.

We will return to the relationship between the decision-making environment and legal conscientiousness in the final chapter. There I will explore the idea that, in terms of securing compliance with administrative law, there is some level of equilibrium between legal conscientiousness and the extent to which judicial review operates as a sanction. There is an interplay between the two which is important to take account of in interpreting and applying the analytical framework of this book. Legal conscientiousness may not be as important for compliance in some decision-making contexts where judicial review has a greater capacity to operate as a sanction. The element of sanction may, to an extent, mitigate the importance of legal conscientiousness for compliance. However, the circumstances where this might happen are few, and the degree of mitigation is limited in any event. Legal conscientiousness will always be important, it is suggested, and, to return to the basic point of this chapter, the decision-making environment has a role to play in determining the extent to which it can flourish.

The basic empirical observation of this chapter—that the decision-making environment can be characterised as an arena in which there is a plurality of normative systems—leads us to the hypothesis which helps us understand the effectiveness of judicial review in securing compliance with administrative law: judicial review's effectiveness will be enhanced where there is no competition between normative systems. The more the demands of the various systems converge with those of law, the greater will be the effectiveness of judicial review. Alternatively, given the fact that a competition between systems is the norm rather than the exception, judicial review's effectiveness will be enhanced by an increased strength of law within the decision-making environment. Assessing an increase or decrease in law's strength is not an easy matter. It should be the subject of continued empirical enquiry and the complexity of decision-making practices revealed by ethnographic studies amplifies the difficulty of fully understanding how law's strength may increase or decrease within the environment. Nevertheless, the substantial body of regulation literature has stressed the importance of three features which may guide this enquiry: the extent to which law may sanction regulatees; the extent to which law may persuade regulatees of its virtues, and the extent to which it may be flexible in switching between these two strategies in response to regulatees.

The next chapter takes forward the theme about competitive models of administrative justice at play in the decision-making environment as part of our consideration of the final element of the administrative realm—the law. The work of Mashaw (1983) in particular is explored in order set up the argument that, just as in the socio-legal literature, so also in legal doctrine is administrative justice a contested term.

Part 4: The Law

Part 4: The Law

6

The Contestedness of
Administrative Justice

THIS NEXT SECTION of the book considers the third element of the
administrative realm—the law. It sets out the final condition
under which judicial review's effectiveness in securing compliance with
administrative law will be maximised. Although we must engage in a
fair amount of detail in justifying this condition, the basic idea is fairly
straightforward. It is that judicial review must give out a consistent
message about what compliance with administrative law requires in
relation to specific areas of governmental decision-making. In other
words, it must not give out conflicting or confusing signals about what
administrative law requires of decision-makers. The clearer and more
consistent the message, the greater will be the chance of judicial review
securing compliance with administrative law.

The condition that judicial review projects a consistent message
about the requirements of administrative law rests on a logical proposition—that if confusing or unclear messages emanate from the court,
government agencies which are trying to comply with the court's
mandate will not know how to act. We noted at the outset of this book
that the term 'administrative law' was being used to refer both to the
common law principles of lawful administration, and to the content of
statutory schemes such as the homelessness law being administered by
the housing authorities which took part in this study. In relation to the
statutory rules of homelessness law, the basic proposition explored
here could simply be stated and no more need be said. If, for example,
in ruling on the extent of accommodation duties, the court swithered
between a view that permanent accommodation must be offered to
'successful' applicants, and a view that non-permanent offers would
suffice to fulfil the duty, this would clearly be confusing for housing
authorities which were conscientiously trying to follow the court's
guidance.

However, there is much more to be said in relation to the common
law requirements of lawful administration, and the bulk of this part of

the book engages with this aspect of administrative law. Daintith and Page have noted (1999: 338) that while judicial review has become more widespread over the years, it is difficult to claim that it has become more predictable, observing that it is an area of law replete with judicial discretion and open-textured standards. This part of the book, and chapters 7 and 8 in particular, make a related point—that the concept of administrative justice is highly contested within administrative law doctrine.

This chapter begins the analysis by illustrating briefly that the meaning of administrative justice is contested within academic literature. Good administration, then, according to administrative justice scholarship, has a number of conceptions. Chapters 7 and 8, which form the bulk of the analysis in this part of the book, engage in a doctrinal analysis of administrative law. This is done in order to demonstrate that, just as in the socio-legal literature, administrative justice is also contested within administrative law doctrine, and, as we shall see, to an extent there are parallels between the doctrinal models and those in some of the socio-legal literature.

Chapters 7 and 8 show that administrative justice is an inherently contested concept in law. The point here is that the common law principles of lawful administration are by their very nature undecided about what administrative law requires. Administrative law is riven by competing priorities and is essentially schizophrenic in character. Its doctrine is sufficiently capacious and flexible that different images of administrative justice can be found within its confines and a fairly detailed treatment of administrative law doctrine is required to demonstrate this point. This character of administrative law significantly intensifies the problem of consistency in comparison with other areas of law. The condition that judicial review provides clear and consistent messages has a particular resonance for administrative law.

Chapter 7 explores the first of two fundamental competitions inherent in administrative law doctrine—that between judicial control and agency autonomy—and chapter 8 explores the second—that between agency and individual interests. In the remainder of this chapter, however, we explore socio-legal administrative justice scholarship.

This chapter picks up where chapter 5 left off—the competition of normative systems within the decision-making environment. In chapter 5 we noted that modern government comprises a regulatory space which is crowded with various formal accountability regimes. These regimes, to an extent, speak to different visions of how the administrative process should unfold. The plurality of accountability regimes testifies to a normative pluralism within the decision-making environment. Administrative justice, in other words, is a contested concept. This is a point which has been made in the socio-legal literature on administrative justice and in the sections below we look more closely at the work of Mashaw and its development by Adler. First, however, a number of preliminary points about the analysis of this chapter need to be made.

Administrative Justice and Administrative Legality

It should be noted at the outset that the concerns of administrative law are wider than those of the socio-legal administrative justice scholarship which will be focused on in this chapter. The work described below is concerned primarily with procedural justice. This is an important element of administrative justice and is obviously a fundamental concern of administrative law—most clearly in relation to the doctrine of procedural fairness. However, administrative law is also concerned with matters which are less procedural and more substantive. The distinction is not watertight and there is certainly a relationship between procedural and substantive matters (Galligan, 1996). However, it is fair to say that administrative law addresses a wider set of issues than that discussed in the administrative justice literature described below. As we shall see further, administrative law additionally makes demands on public agencies, for example, not to overstep the remit given to them by Parliament and to make rational decisions. Nevertheless, it is the contention of this part of the book that, just as the socio-legal scholarship offers competing models of administrative justice, so does administrative law doctrine. There is wide scope for how administrative law principles are applied by the courts and by exploring the case law we can find similarly competing images of administrative justice in this sense. In relation to administrative law doctrine, then, the term 'administrative justice' is being used in a wider sense than it is used in the socio-legal literature surveyed—the phrase 'administrative legality' could easily be substituted. But the contention about the contestedness of the concept is the same, and this is the principal message to be taken from this chapter.

What Activities are Covered by 'Administrative Justice'?

Before exploring in greater depth below the contested character of administrative justice within academic scholarship, two further preliminary notes require to be made. In this subsection, I need to make clear what level of activity is being focused on in using the term 'administrative justice'. My focus is on primary decision-making. Consistent with the aims of this book, 'administrative justice' is used here to refer to normative and legal conceptions of the aims, values and focus of decision-making within government agencies. The questions of what the administrative process should try to achieve and how it should go about achieving it are the end points of the use of the term, rather than just the starting point. The term 'administrative justice' can, of course, be used to encompass the justice inherent in primary decision-making *and* various forms of redress. This is the sense in which the word is used by, for example, Harris and Partington (1999: 2). 'Administrative justice' in this broader sense is looking at the overall architecture of the administrative justice system. However, the aim of this book is to consider the effectiveness of judicial review as a regulator of ongoing, primary decision-making in government agencies. My aim in the following sections, accordingly, is to illustrate the contested character of administrative justice in scholarship which focuses on agency decision-making and the normative debates about how it should be fashioned.

Different Treatments of Administrative Justice in Socio-Legal Scholarship

A final preliminary word should be said about the field of socio-legal administrative justice scholarship. It is perhaps helpful to contrast two distinct approaches to research concerning normative conceptions of administrative justice. On the one hand, there is an analytical approach which seeks to build or dissect normative theories of administrative justice. This kind of work is interesting in and of itself, but may also be used constructively in critiquing conceptions of administrative justice found in popular, political and legal discourses. The work of Galligan (1996) exemplifies this approach. On the other hand, there is research which uses conceptions of administrative justice as a starting point for enquiry, rather than as the end point of enquiry. The work of Mashaw (1983) is an important instance of this second approach. He uses a plurality of critical conceptions of administrative justice as a starting point for the empirical enquiry of welfare administration. An excellent example of similar scholarship in the UK is that of Adler (see Adler, *forthcoming*). Adler and Longhurst (1994), following Mashaw, use a plurality of views on how prison decision-making should occur as a springboard for investigating the social conditions which produce different administrative justice practices in that particular context. Similarly, Adler and Henman (2001) adopt a similar approach to explore the impact of information technology on the development of administrative justice practices in the field of social security administration across twelve jurisdictions.

These two approaches are not suggested as being exhaustive. One might also mention empirical work which investigates citizens' perceptions of administrative justice, based on their experiences of being subject to administrative procedures (for example, Sainsbury, Hurst and Lawton, 1995; Berthoud and Bryson, 1997; Cowan and Halliday, 2003). This work in the field of social welfare, influenced in part by social psychological approaches to procedural justice (for example, Lind and Tyler, 1988; Tyler 1988), is used to inform policy debates and may contribute to normative discussions of administrative justice (though this is doubted by some: see Galligan, 1996: 89–95). Nevertheless, it is the second broad approach to normative conceptions of administrative justice which is adopted in this book. My purpose in this part of the book is to illustrate the contested character of administrative justice in such literature, then to identify some (in some instances related) models of administrative justice within legal doctrine, before going on to assess the ability of judicial review to fashion the administrative process towards its own conceptions of good administration. A plurality of normative conceptions of administrative justice, then, is the starting point for empirical enquiry.

CONCEPTIONS OF ADMINISTRATIVE JUSTICE

In this section I look at some pertinent scholarship which explores the contested character of administrative justice. This is a theme which has been written about quite extensively and explored in a number of contexts, both implicitly (see, for example, Nonet, 1969; Davis, 1969; Handler, 1986; Sossin, 1994) and explicitly (see, for example, Kagan, 1978; Jones, 1989; Ison, 1999; Mulcahy, 1999; Scott, 2000). However, for the ease of my argument, I use here the example of Mashaw's work (1983) and its subsequent development by Adler (forthcoming; Adler and Longhurst, 1994; Adler and Henman, 2001). It is chosen because it offers a particularly clear and instructive illustration of the contestedness of administrative justice (focusing on procedural justice) in relation to primary administrative decision-making.

Mashaw's Models of Administrative Justice

In Mashaw's study of the adjudication of social security disability benefits, he sets out three models of administrative justice, all of which are derived from the critical literature about disability benefits administration in the USA. From this literature, he detects three broad and different perspectives on the goals of the administration and on how it should unfold. The first strand of criticism was that the administration had failed to provide adequate service to claimants. These critics envisaged a stronger role for medical and social services personnel, and suggested that the administration of benefits claims should involve such personnel making professional judgments about how the needs of disabled claimants could best be met. The second strand of criticism focused on the procedural rights of claimants in the decision-making process. It argued that the system was acting unfairly in failing to protect the rights of the individual as the subject of, and participant in, the administrative process. Specific criticisms focused on matters such as the inadequacy of letters of refusal, the lack of adversarial testing of evidence provided by claimants, and so forth. The third strand of criticism focused less directly on the plight of the individual claimant, and more on the functioning of the system as a whole. It suggested that the administrative system was producing inconsistent decisions. It argued for greater internal control and supervision to make the process more predictable and consistent, and less subject to the vagaries of individual offices and officers. Suggestions for remedying the problem included clearer and more comprehensive criteria to guide the exercise of discretion, better systems of managerial oversight, quality assurance, and so forth.

Mashaw believed that these diverse critiques of the workings of the disability benefits administration each reflected distinct conceptions of administrative justice. Mashaw defines administrative justice as meaning 'those qualities of a decision process that provide arguments for the acceptability of its decisions' (1983: 24–25). Accordingly, he constructed a three-fold typology. The models of administrative justice he set out are each attractive in their own right, but are highly competitive: 'the internal logic of any one of them tends to drive the characteristics of the others from the field as it works itself out in concrete situations' (1983: 23). So, on the ground, we may expect to see evidence of each model in action, though one will generally be dominant. The three models are (1) bureaucratic rationality; (2) professional treatment; and (3) moral judgment.

The focus of the bureaucratic rationality model is on the administrative system as a whole (rather than on the individual claimant) and its ability to implement effectively a legislative or policy programme. It is concerned, then, with efficiency—the values of accuracy (targeting benefits to those eligible under the programme) and cost-effectiveness. In devising the programme, legislators or policy makers have decided who is eligible and who is not—it has made the value judgments about deservingness. The task of the administrative system is to implement those preferences on a grand scale in as accurate and consistent a way as possible, and with a concern for economy,

> [t]he legitimating force of this conception flows both from its claim to correct implementation of otherwise legitimate social decisions and from its attempt to realize society's preestablished goals in some particular substantive domain while conserving social resources for the pursuit of other valuable ends. (1983: 26)

Discretionary judgments by individual officers are antithetical to the goals of accuracy and consistency. Instead, the administrative system must operate on the basis of clear rules and guidance which tell low-level officers how to process claims and which promote consistency of decision-making. Systems of internal supervision and control buttress the detail of the rules.

Professional treatment, by way of contrast, has at its heart the service of the client. Medicine is clearly the exemplar. The client comes to a doctor with a self-defined problem and the doctor responds by using his/her professional knowledge and skills to alleviate the problem. In the context of disability benefits administration, this translates into a claimant-centred and needs-based administrative process. The goal of the system is to meet the needs of the individual claimant. The administrative system revolves around the claimant and is about matching available resources to claimants' needs through the medium of professional and clinical judgment. Information about the claimant must be obtained, but accuracy is not really a fundamental concern— or at least not a normative concern. The truth of information provided in the course of a claim matters only in so far as it is important for the improvement of the claimant's welfare. Far more significant is the professional judgment of the decision-maker about what is required to meet the claimant's needs:

> The professional combines the information of others with his or her own observations and experience to reach conclusions that are as much art as science. Moreover, judgment is always subject to revision as conditions change, as attempted therapy proves unsatisfactory or therapeutic successes emerge. The application of clinical judgment entails a relationship and may involve repeated instances of service-oriented decisionmaking . . . Justice lies in having the appropriate professional judgment applied to one's particular situation *in the context of a service relationship*. (emphasis in original) (1983: 28–29)

Mashaw's third model is that of moral judgment (perhaps a confusing title). This model derives from traditional notions of court-centred adjudication. The function of such adjudication is not just to resolve disputes about facts, but is also to decide between the competing interests of litigants—what Mashaw describes as 'value defining' (1983: 29). Issues such as reasonableness, deservingness and responsibility are not questions of fact, but rather are matters of judgment. Accordingly, litigants must be afforded procedural protections in the dispute so that they can have an equal opportunity to present their case, rebut allegations against them, and argue for their interests to be privileged. Further, the decision-maker is traditionally unbiased and passive. In relation to the administration of disability benefits, this translates into an administrative process which is focused on the individual claimant and his/her procedural rights. The adversarial element clearly cannot be transposed over to the context of benefits administration, but in certain respects the claimant is nevertheless treated *as if* he/she is in dispute over a rights claim. The administrative system views the claimant as someone who has come to claim a right, and revolves around giving the claimant a fair opportunity to fully participate in the process of adjudicating whether the right exists or is to be denied. The focus here, once again, is on the claimant rather than on the benefits system as a whole (as in the bureaucratic rationality model). So, the claimant enjoys certain, though not all, of the procedural safeguards afforded in the traditional litigation process. 'The important point is that the "justice" of this model inheres in its promise of a full and equal opportunity to obtain one's entitlements' (1983: 31).

Developments on Mashaw

Mashaw's insights are important and have been highly influential. His thesis about the existence of competing models of administrative justice in relation to administrative decision-making is very valuable, and important for this study. However, there are two points to be made about the detail of the models he sets out. The first is about his model of professional treatment and its general applicability within the world of government administration. The second is about the exhaustiveness of his models.

The Significance of the Professional Treatment Model

It is questionable how significant the professional treatment model is for the normative critique of government administration. Mashaw's was a study of disability benefits administration and this brings with it a particular set of medical and social concerns that resonate clearly for a professional treatment model of administrative justice, but perhaps are unlikely to be replicated very widely within the world of government administration. Although he suggests that the service delivery goal, which is obvious in medicine, is also a defining characteristic of the law, the ministry and social work, it is suggested that the professional treatment model, though clearly relevant to some distinct areas of public service (for example, social work and the health service), is peripheral to the concerns of government administration in general (at least in the UK).[1]

---

[1] For an analysis of the professional treatment model in relation to social security administration in Sweden, see Jewell (2003).

The two key features of the professional treatment model—(1) servicing of a client's needs, and (2) the exercise of professional judgment—are unlikely to combine very often in a critique of contemporary UK government administration.

However, individually, they are very pertinent for arguments about how the administration should operate. A focus on clients' needs has very much been on the agenda since the Citizen's Charter and the advent of customer care in public administration. Similarly, a privileging of professional expertise has long been a concern of administrative law doctrine. These ideas will be developed further below, but for the time being it is sufficient to take from them the suggestion that Mashaw's typology of administrative justice may not be exhaustive. This leads us to the second point to be made about his work.

The Exhaustiveness of Mashaw's Typology

It is important to recognise that Mashaw's typology of administrative justice was written in the USA in 1983. His typology derived from the critical literature around US disability benefits administration. We should not, then, expect his typology to be exhaustive either for all jurisdictions or for all time. Indeed, the job of updating the typology and taking account of developments in governance has been undertaken by Adler (forthcoming); and with Henman (2001). He uses the language of 'ideal types' (2001: 197), rather than models, and adds three new types. They are: (1) managerialism; (2) consumerism; and (3) markets.

Managerialism gives autonomy to public sector managers. Managers bear the responsibility for achieving prescribed standards of service in an efficient way and enjoy the freedom to manage their departments to this end. They are subject to systems of performance audit, and the administrative system revolves around demonstrating the quality of administration according to defined performance indicators. Like Mashaw's bureaucratic rationality model, the focus of this ideal type is on the administrative system as a whole, and only indirectly on the plight of individual citizens (who are presumed to benefit from the attainment of an efficient system).

By way of contrast, the plight of the citizen is at the heart of Adler's consumerism ideal type. Here, the administrative system revolves around producing consumer satisfaction. This involves an active engagement with the citizen as a consumer of public services, and a responsiveness by the administration to dissatisfaction on the part of its consumers. The levels of service to be enjoyed by consumers, the standards of good administration, are often defined in 'customer charters'. In contrast to managerialism, accountability comes from the ground up—from the consumers themselves—through complaints systems.

The final ideal type added by Adler is that of the market. Here the administrative system is driven by the goal of competitiveness. The citizen here is viewed as a rational customer choosing services from a range of providers. The administrative system revolves around making its services as attractive to the customer as possible. Whereas under consumerism the administrative system was accountable to citizens through complaints systems ('voice'), under the market ideal type, the administrative system is accountable to the market itself and subject to the ever present possibility that the citizen will choose another service provider ('exit').

Discussion of Adler's Development of Mashaw

Adler's extension of Mashaw's work is important and illustrates the significant point that new conceptions of administrative justice emerge as the political and social environment develops. His three new ideal types point us towards new developments in governance and their implications for normative critiques of public administration. Nevertheless, a few critical comments can be made. His new ideal types may not, it is suggested, be as distinct and robust as those of Mashaw. Indeed, I suggest that they should be collapsed into one ideal type— consumerism. It is worth noting at the outset that the introduction of managerial autonomy, the Citizen's Charter (and its agency-specific spin-offs), and the marketisation of public services (corresponding to Adler's models of managerialism, consumerism and the market) are all related aspects of a radical alteration of public administration broadly captured by the term 'New Public Management' (see Hood, 1990). The principles of the Citizen's Charter include service standards, choice and consultation, and value for money (see Page, 1999; Drewry, 2000), all of which are consistent with managerialism and the market. Accordingly, it is not certain how much of a tension or trade-off there is between at least some of Adler's ideal types—both within themselves and in relation to those of Mashaw.

To help us think about this, we can break down the notion of an ideal type of administrative justice into two inherent features: (1) the goal ascribed to the administrative process; and (2) the method for achieving the goal. In other words, for the purposes of this analysis, I am simplifying the concept of procedural justice by reducing it to two principal questions: (1) what is the administrative process supposed to achieve? and (2) how should it go about achieving it? Under Mashaw's bureaucratic rationality model, the goal is to implement a policy or legislative programme accurately and efficiently. The method for achieving the goal is to process information elicited from claimants under internal supervision, with the benefit of detailed rules about what information to elicit and how to process it. For the professional treatment model, the goal is to provide a needs-oriented service to the citizen to his/her satisfaction, and the method for achieving the goal is the application of professional or clinical knowledge in dialogue with the client. For the moral judgment model, the goal is to determine a rights claim in a way that is procedurally fair (mimicking, as far as possible, the example of court procedures), and the method for doing this is to afford a number of procedural protections to the claimant so that he/she can fully participate in the decision-making process.

If we turn to Adler, we can see the goal of the market is to match supply with demand, or 'market survival' as I would term it. However, it is unclear in his account what the implications of this are for how the administrative process should be fashioned. Presumably, customer satisfaction would be a fundamental concern, as would economic efficiency. Indeed, it is suggested that the market is better thought of as an umbrella term under which the values of efficiency and customer satisfaction are played out. Efficiency and customer satisfaction *are* market values, and to distinguish 'the market' from them betrays the inherent connections and weakens the analysis. As Harlow and Rawlings have pointed out (1997: 146–47) both managerialism and the Charter programme were introduced to give a market-like discipline to public service providers where a true market was not possible. So, in terms of our analysis of ideal types of administrative justice, and their respective demands on the administrative process, 'the market' should disappear as a distinct model, as its presence is already felt in the models of managerialism and consumerism.

This leads us to an examination of managerialism. The goal here is to implement a legislative or policy scheme efficiently while maintaining specified standards of service. The method for achieving this goal, however, is unclear in Adler's analysis, it is suggested. Within the administrative agency, it seems entirely possible (perhaps likely) that the method would be the same as for bureaucratic rationality: information processing, rules, internal supervision. There are doubts, accordingly, about the degree of tension between the model of managerialism and Mashaw's model of bureaucratic rationality. Both of these, as already noted, focus on efficiency. It is certainly true that the mode of *control* over the administration is different between the two ideal types: there is greater managerial autonomy under managerialism. Also, the standards of efficiency may be more clearly (and externally) defined under managerialism than under bureaucratic rationality, but the essential goals which drive and inform day-to-day administration are much the same. Adler suggests that the mode of decision-making for managerialism is 'managerial autonomy', but this speaks more to the structuring of the public agency and the form of accountability than to the method of achieving programme implementation and efficiency on a routine basis on the ground. Managerialism certainly represents a new structure for providing incentives to public agencies to be efficient in programme implementation, but as a model of administrative justice it is better regarded as being a contemporary gloss on Mashaw's bureaucratic rationality. It too should disappear, then, as a distinct model of administrative justice.

In relation to consumerism, however, Adler has certainly captured something new and distinct. Consumerism and the rise of 'customer care' seems to represent a new normative model for fashioning the administrative process. Like Mashaw's moral judgment and professional treatment models, the focus is on the individual as the subject of the administrative process. However, in contrast to the moral judgment model, the concern is with customer satisfaction rather than procedural fairness; and in contrast with professional treatment, customer satisfaction is achieved through customer care, rather than through the application of professional or clinical knowledge. Under the professional treatment model the individual is treated as a person in need, whereas under consumerism the individual is treated as if a rational economic actor (Baron and Scott, 1992). Consumerism's constellation of values such as courtesy, helpfulness, promptness, openness, responsiveness, plain language, etc, are aimed at meeting the needs of the *customer* and so are independent of (and prior to) his/her substantive needs or desires. In a sense, they relate to the 'process' needs of the individual who engages with a government agency, but represent a distinct set of values to those of procedural fairness. They pull the administration in a new and different direction.[2]

It should be noted, of course, that Adler discusses a further layer of enquiry in relation to ideal types of administrative justice: forms of redress. He suggest forms of redress which are characteristic of the various ideal types of administrative justice. They demonstrate the distinctiveness of each: for Mashaw's bureaucratic rationality, the remedy is administrative review; for professional treatment, complaint to a professional body; for moral judgment, appeal to a court or tribunal; for managerialism, complaint to management (or regulatory body); for consumerism, 'voice' and/or compensation through a Charter; and finally for market, 'exit' and/or court action for breach of contract or compensation. These insights are important. However, the concern of this chapter is to focus on conceptions of administrative justice in relation to primary decision-making. Although there are clear differences between the various ideal types' characteristic forms of redress, this should not distract us from a focus on the implications of the differing conceptions of administrative justice for how government agencies should fashion their administrative processes. It is at this level that Adler's work, though offering important advances, does not offer as complete, robust and distinctive ideal types as those of Mashaw; though, as I have argued above, his ideal type of 'consumerism' offers a new model of administrative justice which should be added to Mashaw's typology.

CONCLUSION

Regardless of whether one agrees with either the detail of Adler's work, or my critique of it, the important point to take from this discussion is that there are competing normative views about the goals of the administrative process and the best way of achieving those goals. We touched upon this point in the previous chapter's discussion of the plurality of accountability regimes in the regulatory space of government, and have developed it more fully in this chapter by exploring the work of Mashaw and Adler. The work of both Mashaw and Adler is rooted in an understanding of debates about government among political,

---

[2] This is illustrated to an extent by one of the case studies in Cowan and Halliday's research on homelessness decision-making (2003: 82–87).

academic and stakeholder groups. Inevitably, therefore, the landscape of the normative debates around government administration will be varied and, indeed, will change over time. The contention of the next two chapters is that administrative law doctrine, at least to an extent, reflects this normative pluralism.

7

Judicial Control and Agency Autonomy

INTRODUCTION

T HE AIM OF the next two chapters is to demonstrate that administrative law doctrine is sufficiently capacious and flexible to accom-
modate several competing images of administrative justice. The basic
argument here is that administrative law is structured around two parallel tensions or competitions. First, there is a competition between the
interests, on the one hand, of the public agency which has the task of
administering law, and on the other, of the individual who is the subject of the administrative process. This competition is played out most
clearly in relation to the doctrine of procedural fairness, though is also
evidenced, as we shall see, in relation to other doctrines. The second
competition is between judicial control, on the one hand, and agency
autonomy on the other. This is a basic constitutional struggle about
who gets to decide what, and is most obviously played out in relation
to the legal doctrines concerning error of law, though, similarly, it is
evidenced elsewhere. It is also framed in the more pragmatic (and
related) terms of the relative expertise of public agencies and the courts.

These two basic tensions in administrative law permit the court to
develop competing models of administrative justice—competing
images, on the one hand, of whose interests should be privileged in the
administrative process, and on the other, of who gets to decide what.
From a normative perspective, these competitions may be regarded as
what provide administrative law with its inherent and beneficial flexibility (see, for example, Galligan, 1996). However, more practically,
from an administrator's point of view, they comprise the inherent
contingency and uncertainty of administrative law.

The Study of Administrative Law

The next two chapters will engage in a legal analysis of administrative law. A number of the doctrines of administrative law will be examined in order to demonstrate their flexibility and to illustrate the two parallel competitions within the case law and so the competing images of administrative justice. The study of administrative law doctrine is now, of course, a weighty undertaking. The importance of the subject for citizens' lives is matched by the extent of the case law and the scale of the scholarly works in the field. The major works (for example, de Smith, Woolf and Jowell, 1995; Clyde and Edwards, 2000; Wade and Forsyth, 2000; Craig, 2003) are voluminous, to say the least. It is clearly not possible in a study of this kind to do justice to the vast array of legal sources or to the rich and detailed doctrinal analyses which contribute to administrative law scholarship. Such work is considerably beyond the scope of this book. Nevertheless, it should be possible to engage in an overview of administrative law doctrine to the extent that we can begin to see different models of administrative justice in the flexibility of the doctrines and the scope of the court's powers of review.

Before I embark on this task, however, a brief word should be offered about how the grounds of review should be categorised. The potential avenues for attacking administrative decisions are many. The increase in judicial review litigation (charted in Bridges, Meszaros and Sunkin, 1996) has meant that the case law is now vast and the doctrines of administrative law—at least the detail of them—rather complex. There are a number of ways of categorising the grounds of judicial review. A quick glance at some of the leading texts reveals this. Additionally, of course, the courts themselves categorise the grounds of review in different ways, although Lord Diplock's three-fold division in the *GCHQ* case[1] (illegality, irrationality and procedural impropriety) is probably still the most significant. It is easy, then, for a student of administrative law—or even a scholar for that matter—to be intimidated by the difficulty of the task of trying to impose a coherent structure on the grounds of review. However, there is an important (and perhaps comforting) point to be taken from this, and it is made time after time by the courts and commentators: the grounds of judicial review are not watertight and mutually exclusive, but rather overlap

---

[1] *Council for Civil Service Unions v Minister for the Civil Service* [1985] AC 374.

and bleed into each other.[2] This changes the job of describing the grounds of review from one of finding the right classification to one of finding an appropriate classification for the task in hand. There is no right answer, in other words. As Clyde and Edwards have noted (2000: 441),

> the attempt to formulate precise categories may be frustrated by the cross-flow of those basic ideas and the imprecision of the concepts usually used to identify one ground from another.

As a way into the legal analysis, I have generated a general categorisation of the grounds of review which attempts to capture the principal concerns of administrative law (though this scheme may not be regarded as orthodox by some). Broadly speaking, it is suggested, we can see that the courts concern themselves with six principal issues which are reasonably (though not completely) distinct: (1) whether administrative bodies have exceeded or delegated the powers granted to them; (2) whether the decision-maker has made an error of law; (3) whether decision-making processes are rational (ie, whether there is a sufficiently rational connection between the decision made and the means of getting there); (4) whether decision-making processes are fair; (5) whether decision-outcomes are substantively rational; (6) whether the decision process or outcome breaches a human right or a right under EU law.

The various grounds of review can be seen as contributing towards these six goals. The classic, narrow ultra vires doctrine is concerned with whether public agencies are acting within, and not exceeding their legal powers or capacity. (Where, for example, they have been given power to provide a ferry service across a river, they may not use the stand-by ferry boats for pleasure excursions[3]). The rule against the delegation of decision-making similarly relates to the powers of public agencies. Here the concern is that powers which have been granted by Parliament to a particular body are not then sub-delegated to someone else. The doctrine of error of law stands on its own feet as a broad category of review (though historically has been subject to a preliminary and rather complex concern with the powers or 'jurisdiction' of public bodies). The rule against the fettering of discretion relates to the

---

[2] See, for example, the dictum of Lord Greene MR in *Associated Provincial Picture Houses Ltd v Wednesbury Corporation* [1948] 1 KB 223, and that of Lord Hailsham in *London and Clydeside Estates Ltd v Aberdeen District Council* 1980 SC (HL) 1.

[3] *D and J Nicol v Dundee Harbour Trustees* 1915 SC (HL) 7.

rationality of the decision-making process, as do the rules concerning consideration of relevant (and only relevant) facts and the rule against improper purposes. The fair hearing principle and the rule against bias relate primarily to the fairness of administrative procedures (though the rule against bias may also be regarded as being related to the rationality of the decision process). The doctrines of proportionality and *Wednesbury* unreasonableness (or irrationality) relate to the substantive rationality of decision outcomes. The heading of review regarding the breach of the Human Rights Act 1998 or EU law is an overarching and self-explanatory category.

The scheme above is offered as a way of capturing, from a high vantage point, the essential goals of administrative law. This is offered simply as a helpful starting point before we engage in legal analysis. However, the analysis which follows will not stand or fall on the categorisation adopted. The more important point of this chapter and the next is to demonstrate that the two sets of tensions within administrative law produce different images of how administrative agencies should go about making decisions. We can now go on to consider how these competitions are evidenced in the grounds of review. It should be noted that, in order to demonstrate the two basic competitions, not all the principles of administrative law need to be discussed. The legal analysis is intended to be illustrative rather than exhaustive. The discussion will focus on principles falling within the headings of error of law, procedural rationality, procedural fairness and substantive rationality. It is hoped that this analysis will be sufficient to make persuasive the overall argument about the plurality of images of administrative justice within administrative law.

We can proceed now to the exploration of the first competition within administrative law which is between judicial control and agency autonomy.

COMPETITION BETWEEN JUDICIAL CONTROL AND AGENCY AUTONOMY

Introduction

The competition between judicial control and agency autonomy (Craig, 2003: 510) goes to the heart of administrative law. This is a constitutional tension which is sometimes framed in terms of the separation of powers doctrine, but is also framed (relatedly) in terms of the respective expertise of the public agency and the courts. What is at issue here is who gets to decide what—what are the respective roles of the administration and the courts in resolving aspects of an administrative decision, or, indeed, the ultimate decision outcome?

A word of clarification should be offered at this stage. There is a clear and obvious sense in which the courts always get the final say. Even where the court holds that the administrative agency should resolve an issue within its own discretion, it is the court which has the authority to make this preliminary decision. But this is to say no more than that the question of 'who should decide what?' is a justiciable question. The focus and concern of this chapter is about the message regarding decision-making which is conveyed to administrative agencies through judicial review. Where a court holds that decision-making authority rests with the administrative agency, the message about agency autonomy and discretion is conveyed to the agency, even though that message emanates from a judicial decision. What is of significance is that the court is indicating to the agency that it is holding back its own power to interfere with the decision-making process, to resolve certain matters itself, and impose a single judicial standard on a given question. By doing this, the courts permit the agency to follow its instincts and preferences, and to have confidence in the finality of its judgements, secure in the knowledge that the court will not scrutinise agency discretion according to judicial preferences, but will do so, instead, according to a much more remote standard of reasonableness. Rather than looking externally to the courts for interpretations of words or phrases or for guidance about how they should resolve comparable questions, agencies can be more introspective, develop their expertise and enjoy the broad scope of their own discretion.

Having clarified this issue, we can now examine the tension as it plays out in the jurisprudence of the courts. The case law concerning a number of the grounds of judicial review demonstrates this competition. To begin this analysis, we can look at the grounds of review concerned with the substantive rationality of decision-outcomes.

Substantive Rationality of Decision-Outcomes

Unreasonableness

In addition to being concerned with the rationality of the decision-making process, administrative law is also concerned with substantive decision outcomes, or the merits of the decision as it is sometimes phrased. Although the courts express a reluctance to interfere with the merits of decisions, they may do so if the outcome is perverse. The test of perversity was most famously described by Lord Greene MR in *Associated Provincial Picture Houses Ltd v Wednesbury Corporation*[4] as being whether a decision was 'so unreasonable that no reasonable authority could ever have come to it.' This category of perversity, known as '*Wednesbury* unreasonableness', has also been termed 'irrationality' by Lord Diplock in the *GCHQ* case.[5] He described the test as being whether the decision was[6]

> so outrageous in its defiance of logic or of accepted moral standards that no sensible persons who had applied his mind to the question to be decided could have arrived at it.

This high threshold test for interference with the merits of decisions reflects a more general constitutional position regarding the separate functions of the judiciary and the administration. Under the separation of powers doctrine it is generally not for the judiciary to exercise the discretion which has been entrusted by Parliament to the executive. One element of this position is the view that the courts and the executive have separate expertise (Barber, 2001). The courts consistently stress that they are not in the best position to make some of the difficult choices and decisions which administrative agencies have to make. Administrative agencies are closer to the ground and have built up experience in making such decisions. Both aspects of the courts' general reluctance to interfere with merits—separation of powers, and deference to executive expertise—can be seen, for example, in the judgment of Lord Greene MR in *Wednesbury*:[7]

---

[4] [1948] 1 KB 223.
[5] *Council for Civil Service Unions v Minister for the Civil Service* [1985] AC 374.
[6] [1985] AC 374 at p 410.
[7] [1948] 1 KB 223 at p 230.

Once it is conceded, as it must be conceded in this case, that the particular subject-matter dealt with by this condition was one which it was competent for the authority to consider, there, in my opinion, is an end of the case. Once that is granted, Mr Gallop is bound to say that the decision of the authority is wrong because it is unreasonable, and in saying that he is really saying that the ultimate arbiter of what it and is not reasonable is the court and not the local authority. It is just there, it seems to me, that the argument breaks down. It is clear that the local authority are entrusted by Parliament with the decision on a matter which the knowledge and experience of that authority can best be trusted to deal with.

Similarly, in relation to the review of policy decisions, Lord Diplock in the GCHQ case noted:[8]

The reasons for the decision maker taking one course rather than another do not normally involve questions to which, if disputed, the judicial process is adapted to provide the right answer, by which I mean that the kind of evidence that is admissible under judicial procedures and the way in which it has to be adduced tend to exclude from the attention of the court competing policy considerations which, if the executive discretion is to be wisely exercised, need to be weighed against one another—a balancing exercise which judges by their upbringing and experience are ill-qualified to perform.

The ground of irrationality is, like all the grounds of review, subject to a variable intensity of application. As Clyde and Edwards have noted (2000: 570):

The standard required to meet irrationality is not a universal one and must vary with the circumstances so that what is irrational for one decision maker may not be for another. In other words, the approach to irrationality will require deference in some cases and stricter scrutiny in other cases.

The variable intensity with which this test is applied has meant that the courts have interfered with administrative decisions which seem to fall below the high threshold outlined in *Wednesbury*. A few examples can illustrate this. In *Hall & Co Ltd v Shoreham-by-Sea Urban District Council*[9] a planning authority imposed a condition of planning permission that the applicant should build a road on their property at their own expense and grant a public right of way over it. An alternative means of constructing the road was available to the council where compensation would have been paid to the property owner. The condition imposed was held to be *Wednesbury* unreasonable. Similarly, in *West*

---

[8] [1985] AC 374 at p 410.
[9] [1964] 1 WLR 240.

Glamorgan County Council v Rafferty,[10] a local authority which had failed in its duty under the Caravan Sites Act 1968 to provide a site for gypsies raised an action to recover possession of council property on which gypsies were squatting, asserting that the gypsies were causing a nuisance. The decision to seek possession was held to be *Wednesbury* unreasonable. Further, in the case of *R (on the application of Wulfsohn) v Legal Services Commission*,[11] the Funding Review Committee of the Legal Services Committee revoked an applicant's entitlement to legal aid because he failed to produce requested information from the Benefits Agency. The applicant had written to the Benefits Agency seeking the information but had failed to chase it any further. The information was not produced within the timescale granted by the Legal Services Commission. The decision to revoke entitlement to legal aid under these circumstances was similarly held to be *Wednesbury* unreasonable.

Each of the administrative decisions in the above cases seem unreasonable. And, indeed, one might be able to imagine other legal grounds for attacking them. However, it is doubtful, it is suggested, whether they are unreasonable in the *Wednesbury* sense: *so* unreasonable that *no* reasonable decision-maker would have made the same decision. In such instances, the courts seem to be employing a less extreme sense of 'unreasonable'. This lowering of the threshold in practice has now been matched by a more modest re-articulation of the test in the House of Lords in the case of *R v Chief Constable of Sussex ex parte International Trader's Ferry Ltd*.[12] Lord Cooke in this case stated:

> [The *Wednesbury* case], an apparently briefly-considered case, might well not be decided the same way today; and the judgment of Lord Greene MR twice uses . . . the tautologous formula 'so unreasonable that no reasonable authority could ever have come to it.' Yet judges are entirely accustomed to respecting the proper scope of administrative discretions. In my respectful opinion they do not need to be warned off the course by admonitory circumlocutions. When, in *Secretary of State for Education and Science v Tameside Metropolitan Borough Council* [1977] AC 1014, the precise meaning of 'unreasonably' in an administrative context was crucial to the decision, the five speeches in the House of Lords, the three judgments in the Court of Appeal and the two judgments in the Divisional Court all succeeded in avoiding needless complexity. The simple test used throughout

10   [1987] 1 WLR 457.
11   [2001] EWHC Admin 409.
12   [1999] 2 AC 418.

was whether the decision in question was one which a reasonable authority could reach.

The point Lord Cooke is making here is that an exaggerated test is not required to restrain the courts from interfering with the merits of decisions. Judges are capable of restraining themselves with a more modest test of reasonableness. However, it is certainly the case that the extent to which they restrain their powers to decide on the merits varies. Although in some cases (inevitably) there is no explicit rationale for a greater intensity of review, there is, on the whole, an accepted justification expressed in the case law. Where a breach of fundamental rights is in issue, the courts are more willing to interfere with the merits of decisions. In *R v Secretary of State for the Home Department, ex parte Brind*,[13] for example, Lord Templeman asserted the need to go beyond the *Wednesbury* principles in cases of a breach of human rights:[14]

> The subject-matter and the date of the *Wednesbury* principles cannot in my opinion make it either necessary or appropriate for the courts to judge the validity of an interference with human rights by asking themselves whether the Home Secretary has acted irrationally or perversely. It seems to me that the courts cannot escape from asking themselves only whether a reasonable Secretary of State, on the material before him, could reasonably conclude that the interference with freedom of expression which he determined to impose was justifiable.

The underlying reasons which support this interference are (1) separation of powers, and (2) expertise. The courts regard questions of fundamental rights as falling within both their constitutional remit[15] and their expertise. For example, Sir Thomas Bingham MR in *R v Minister of Defence ex parte Smith*, a case concerned with the dismissal of homosexuals from the armed forces on the grounds of their sexuality, observed:[16]

> It is not the constitutional role of the court to regulate the conditions of service in the armed forces of the Crown, nor has it the expertise to do so. But it has the constitutional role and duty of ensuring that the rights of citizens are not abused by the unlawful exercise of executive power. While the court

---

[13] [1991] 1 AC 696.

[14] [1991] 1 AC 696 at p 751.

[15] This position, of course, has been consolidated following the enactment of the Human Rights Act 1998.

[16] [1996] QB 517, at p 556.

must properly defer to the expertise of responsible decision-makers, it must not shrink from its fundamental duty to 'do right to all manner of people. . . .'

The doctrine of *Wednesbury* unreasonableness, or irrationality, then, displays the competition between the judiciary and the administration about who gets the final say about decisions outcomes, even where the decision-making *process* cannot be flawed. Traditionally, the courts have expressed considerable reluctance to retain the final say for themselves. This is justified on constitutional grounds, though a significant part of this reasoning relates the expertise of the government agency in developing policy and making decisions on the ground. However, at the same time, the courts have shown themselves willing at times to exert their power to interfere with the merits of decisions, particularly where fundamental rights are at issue. What we can see in relation to this doctrine is a dominant 'expert' model of decision-making where the courts generally defer to agency expertise, though on occasion keep the decision for themselves.

Disproportionality

A brief word should be added at this point about the doctrine of proportionality. This is another avenue through which the courts explicitly concern themselves with substantive decision-outcomes. The doctrine permits the courts to strike down decisions which constitute disproportionate actions when related to the underlying aim of the decision in question. Proportionality is a doctrine of European law and not, traditionally, of domestic administrative law. However, the grounds of review are not fixed for all time and may be expanded as required.[17] There has been much speculation about whether it might find its way into domestic administrative law as a separate heading of judicial review (see, for example, Jowell and Lester, 1988; Craig 2003: 618–22; Wade and Forsyth, 2000: 368–70). The House of Lords has stated that proportionality is not yet part of the domestic law,[18] but could become one in the future,[19] and individual judges have called for

---

[17] *R v Inland Revenue Commissioners ex parte national Federation of Self-Employed and Small Businesses Ltd* [1982] AC 617; *West v Secretary of State for Scotland* 1992 SC 385.

[18] *R v Secretary of State for the Home Department ex parte Brind* [1991] 1 AC 696.

[19] *Council for Civil Service Unions v Minister for the Civil Service* [1985] AC 374.

its recognition as a principle of domestic law.[20] It certainly is now, however, where human rights are at issue. Following the Human Rights Act 1998, administrative decisions are flawed where they infringe a human right under the European Convention on Human Rights. Many of the human rights are framed in terms which permit limitations on the rights in certain circumstances. For example, freedom of expression under Article 10 may be limited so far as is 'necessary in a democratic society' or in the 'interests of national security' and so on. In applying these tests, the courts will employ the doctrine of proportionality. The same applies where the domestic courts are interpreting European law. However, as with *Wednesbury* unreasonableness, proportionality will be applied with varying intensity. Indeed, Lord Slynn has suggested that the flexibility in its application substantially reduces the difference between the proportionality test and the *Wednesbury* test.[21] The margin of appreciation granted to the administration varies according to context and permits the doctrine of proportionality similarly to be a site of contestation between the judiciary and the administration over who gets to decide on the merits of decisions.

Another site of the competition between judicial control and agency autonomy is the doctrine of error of law. Indeed, the competition here is perhaps more polarised and stark, and it is to this that we now turn.

Error of law

The heading of 'error of law' has a complicated history, having now been freed from its connection to a rather tortured set of concerns over the 'jurisdiction' of public agencies.[22] This is not the place to engage in a proper examination of this history (see, for example, Craig, 2003: chapter 15). However, given the historical relationship between error of law and questions of 'jurisdiction', it is perhaps worth pausing for a moment to draw the distinction between two senses of the word 'jurisdiction', to demonstrate why error of law may now be considered in

---

[20] Lord Slynn in *R (on the Application of Alconbury Developments Ltd) v Secretary of State for Environment, Transport and the Regions* [2001] HRLR 45.

[21] *R v Chief Constable of Sussex ex parte International Trader's Ferry Ltd* [1999] 2 AC 418; *R (on the Application of Alconbury Developments Ltd) v Secretary of State for Environment, Transport and the Regions* [2001] HRLR 45.

[22] See *Anisminic Ltd v Foreign Compensation Commission* [1969] 2 AC 147; *R v Hull University Visitor ex parte Page* [1993] AC 682.

isolation as a head of review, and why this analysis distinguishes it from the courts' concerns with the 'powers' of public bodies.

The ground of review relating to the 'powers' of public bodies (category (1) in the schema offered above) refers here to the narrow concern with whether public bodies exceed their legal mandate—classic, narrow ultra vires. The question is one of legal competence or capacity—whether the public body has been granted the power to act. Does, for example, a local authority which has been put under a duty to provide wholesome water also have the legal mandate to add fluoride in order to improve the dental health of its population?[23] Writ large, the question would become, for example, whether the Scottish Parliament has the power to pass certain legislation.

Error of law, on the other hand, is a broad heading which has replaced 'jurisdiction' (in another, though related, sense of the word) as a controlling principle of review. Until fairly recently, a distinction was drawn between jurisdictional and non-jurisdictional errors of law. The difficult question was whether or not the question of law was integral to the public body's jurisdiction—its power to decide. If it was, the court had a role in reviewing and correcting any errors. If it did not, the court had no role. The House of Lords, however, has now held that all errors law may be reviewed and corrected by the courts.[24] Error of law is no longer subject to a prior question of jurisdiction and therefore stands on its own feet as a head of review. 'Jurisdiction' can now, it is suggested, be regarded as relating to the narrower question of the power to act (legal mandate). The question of whether a public body has exceeded its powers in this sense could, of course, be framed in terms of 'error of law'.[25] The public body could be described as having made an error of law in interpreting its power too expansively. But it has greater explanatory power, it is suggested, to separate out error of law from an excess of legal mandate.

[23] *McColl v Strathclyde Regional Council* 1983 SLT 616. See also *Credit Suisse v Allerdale MBC* [1997] QB 306; *R v Somerset CC ex parte Fewings* [1995] 1 WLR 1037; *Credit Suisse v Waltham Forest LBC* [1997] QB 362.

[24] *R v Hull University Visitor ex parte Page* [1993] AC 682. The position in Scotland, it should be noted, is the same as the English position prior to *Page*. Jurisdiction is still an organising principle in relation to errors of law. See *Watt v Lord Advocate* 1979 SC 120.

[25] Indeed, error of law and narrow ultra vires could be subsumed within the heading of 'illegality': see the dictum of Lord Diplock in *Council for Civil Service Unions v Minister for the Civil Service* [1985] AC 374.

Having made this clarification, we can now consider a key issue within the doctrine of error of law which demonstrates the fundamental tension between judicial authority and agency autonomy.

Questions of Fact and Law

As we have just observed, since the *Page* decision, the courts have gathered all questions of law within their jurisdiction. Where, for example, an administrative decision-maker has misinterpreted a statutory term, or asked itself the wrong question in applying a legal concept, the courts may now interfere with the decision and quash it. The distinction between questions of fact and questions of law (and hence the dividing line between judicial control and agency autonomy) has exercised a number of legal commentators. The fear of some is that judges resolve the law-fact question for reasons that lack analytic rigour (though Endicott (1998) has offered a strong defence). Be that as it may, the courts are capable of applying differing standards to their exercise of this power of interference. Two approaches seem to be present in the case law. First, the courts have treated as a question of law the application of primary facts to a situation to see if it fits a statutory term.[26] This is best explained by way of example. Where, for example, the question is whether someone's living situation amounts to 'accommodation' under the homelessness legislation, the primary facts would comprise the size of a room/property occupied, the availability of amenities, the condition of the living space, the number of persons occupying a room, the occupants' tenure, and so forth. But simply narrating these primary facts does not tell us whether the living space amounts to 'accommodation' under the Act in question. This requires the application of the primary facts to the statutory concept of 'accommodation'. This process, according to the first approach, makes 'accommodation' a question of law.

However, in other instances, the courts have shown great unwillingness to divest government agencies of the discretion to decide such questions themselves. Because all errors of law are now reviewable, to regard all questions of application (which litter public law statutes) as questions of law, would result in the courts taking on a very large workload and power of decision. So, instead the courts have treated

---

[26] See, for example, *Farmer v Cotton's Trustees* [1915] AC 922; *Quiltotex Co Ltd v Minister of Housing and Local Government and Another* [1966] 1 QB 704; *Woodhouse v Brotherhood Ltd* [1972] QB 520; *R v Barnet LBC Ex p Shah* [1983] 2 AC 309.

many questions of applications as questions of fact, unless the public body's determination is unreasonable—and this, it is suggested, seems to be the stronger line of authority.[27] In other words, the courts afford public bodies a wide margin of discretion in applying primary facts to statutory concepts. It is only if they cross a line of reasonableness that the courts will intervene and regard the matter as a question of law. Lord Radcliffe in *Edwards v Bairstow*[28] stated:

> If the case contains anything ex facie which is bad law and which bears upon the determination, it is, obviously, erroneous in point of law. But, without any such misconception appearing ex facie, it may be that the facts found are such that no person acting judicially and properly instructed as to the relevant law could have come to the determination under appeal. In those circumstances, too, the court must intervene. It has no option but to assume that there has been some misconception of the law and that, this has been responsible for the determination. So there, too, there has been error in point of law. I do not think that it much matters whether this state of affairs is described as one in which there is no evidence to support the determination or as one in which the evidence is inconsistent with and contradictory of the determination, or as one in which the true and only reasonable conclusion contradicts the determination. Rightly understood, each phrase propounds the same test. For my part, I prefer the last of the three . . .

A good example of this kind of approach can be seen in the case of *R v Hillingdon LBC ex parte Puhlhofer*[29] where the House of Lords considered the situation used as an example above: whether someone's living situation amounted to 'accommodation' under the homelessness legislation. It held that it was for the local housing authority to determine whether housing applicants were occupying 'accommodation' as a question of fact (in Puhlhofer's case, a room in a guesthouse occupied by two adults and two children):

> What is properly to be regarded as accommodation is a question of fact to be decided by the local authority. There are no rules. Clearly some places in which a person might choose or be constrained to live could not properly be regarded as accommodation at all; it would be a misuse of language to describe Diogenes as having occupied accommodation within the meaning of the Act . . . Where the existence or non-existence of a fact is left to the judgment and discretion of a public body and that fact involves a broad

---

[27] *Edwards v Bairstow* [1956] AC 14; *Ransom v Higgs* [1974] 1 WLR 1594; *R v Hillingdon LBC ex parte Puhlhofer* [1986] 1 AC 484.

[28] [1956] AC 14 at 36.

[29] [1986] 1 AC 484.

spectrum ranging from the obvious to the debatable to the just conceivable, it is the duty of the court to leave the decision of that fact to the public body to whom Parliament has entrusted the decision-making power save in a case where it is obvious that the public body, consciously or unconsciously, are acting perversely.[30]

What we can see here is the courts affording public bodies in certain circumstances a wide margin of discretion, comparable to that afforded under the *Wednesbury* test already discussed above. Some questions of application are for public bodies to determine, so long as the determination is not beyond the realm of reasonableness—perversity in Lord Brightman's words. Lord Brightman expressed concern over the volume of homelessness judicial review applications, calling for the courts to grant leave to apply for judicial review less frequently. In his view, the proper division of labour between government and the courts in relation to implementing homelessness law was that responsibility should lie with the local housing authority. Although there was clearly concern over the plight of the High Court in terms of its administration of justice, Lord Brightman was also articulating his conception of the appropriate separation of powers in relation to homelessness administration. *Puhlhofer* provides an excellent example of how the law-fact distinction captures the competition within administrative law between judicial control and agency autonomy. As Endicott has noted (1998: 294), 'the most common use of the notion of questions of law is to distribute decision-making power and responsibility'.

The variant practice of the courts over questions of application raises the question of what justifies the ascription of question of fact to some issues and not to others. A number of commentators suggest that, generally speaking, there is little observable logic to the patterns of decision-making, criticising the courts for inconsistency (see, for example, Beatson, 1984: 39–45; Craig, 2003: 489; Wade and Forsyth 2000: 922), although the courts do seem more willing to accord 'question of fact' status to issues where the public body is exercising some kind of expertise.[31] Nevertheless, the doctrine of error of law and the law-fact distinction clearly is an area of administrative law where the courts have broad discretion to project competing images of administrative justice: the first where the courts should take control and resolve

---

[30] per Lord Brightman at pp 517–18.
[31] See, for example, *R v Industrial Injuries Commissioner ex parte Amalgamated Engineering Union (No 2)* [1966] 2 QB 31; *Express and Star Ltd v Bunday* [1988] ICR 379.

matters as questions of law, and the second where Parliament is deemed to have given wide discretion to public bodies to exercise judgment, relying on their own expertise, substantially free from interference.

Rationality of Decision-Making Process

Our discussion about the competition between judicial control and agency autonomy may be concluded with a brief glance at how the courts treat statutory requirements regarding the rationality of the decision-making process.

Statutory Requirements about Fact-finding

In addition to common law requirements about decision-making procedures (discussed further below), statutes sometimes provide specific standards concerning the investigations and fact-finding activities which public bodies undertake before decision-making. Such requirements can also be a site of competition between judicial control and agency autonomy. A good example can be found within homelessness law. Under section 62 of the Housing Act 1985, local housing authorities were under a duty to make such enquiries are were necessary to satisfy themselves about whether a housing applicant was, for example, intentionally homeless. In *R v Royal Borough of Kensington & Chelsea ex parte Bayani*, the Court of Appeal held that local authorities should enjoy a wide discretion as to what the term 'necessary' entailed. Lord Justice Neill stated:[32]

> The court should not intervene merely because it considers that further inquiries would have been sensible or desirable. It should intervene only if no reasonable housing authority could have been satisfied on the basis of the inquiries made.

However, the court has not always exercised such restraint in relation to this aspect of homelessness administration and instead have determined substantively themselves whether factual enquiries were adequate.[33] This tension within the case law reflects and embodies the

[32] 22 HLR 406 at p 415.
[33] See, for example, *R v London Borough of Tower Hamlets ex parte Hoque*, *The Times*, 20 July 1993. These cases are discussed further in Halliday (1996).

wider tension between judicial control and agency autonomy. Following *Bayani*, housing authorities may enjoy considerable flexibility about how extensive their enquiries can be regarding housing applicants' histories and circumstances. Under this 'agency autonomy' model of administrative justice, public bodies may rest secure in the knowledge that the courts will only interfere with their practices if they cross a line of perversity. However, the courts have not always been consistent on this question, and instead may promote a 'judicial control' model of decision-making where considerable discretion to resolve such matters is retained, requiring (in theory at least) the public bodies to follow the lead of the courts in implementing the law.

CONCLUSION

This chapter has introduced our legal analysis of administrative law and has suggested that two fundamental competitions exist within the doctrine which render the demands of administrative law uncertain and contingent on context. This focuses our attention on the requirement that the courts give out consistent and clear messages about what administrative law requires in relation to different kinds of decision-making. This argument is continued in chapter 8 when we explore the second basic competition in administrative law—that between agency and individual interests.

8

The Competition between Individual and Agency Interests

H AVING EXPLORED IN the previous chapter the competition evidenced in administrative law doctrine between judicial control
and agency autonomy, this chapter goes on to complete the legal analysis by examining a second fundamental competition: about whose
interests (the individual *vs* the public agency) should be privileged in
the administrative process. The competition is displayed in a number
of the doctrines of administrative law, but is perhaps most clearly
evidenced in relation to procedural fairness, and it is with this doctrine
that the analysis begins.

PROCEDURAL FAIRNESS

Procedural fairness represents, perhaps, the classic case of the flexibility of administrative law doctrine. Indeed, Harlow and Rawlings
characterise it as a 'flexible friend' (1997: 495).[1] The courts have
consistently stressed that procedural fairness requires the application
of a set of principles to particular situations, rather than being a fixed
standard.[2] Lord Bridge, for example, in *Lloyd v McMahon*[3] noted that
the rules of procedural fairness were 'not engraved on tablets of stone'.
Rather, its demands depended on the character of the decision-making
body, the kind of decision being made and the statutory or other framework within which the decision-maker was working. Similarly, Lord
Mustill observed in *R v Home Secretary ex parte Doody*[4] that,

> [t]he principles of fairness are not to be applied by rote identically in every
> situation. What fairness demands is dependent on the context of the
> decision, and this is to be taken into account in all its aspects.

[1] See also Mullan (1975); Craig (1993); Clyde and Edwards (2000: 506).
[2] See, for example, *Russell v Duke of Norfolk* [1949] 1 All ER 109.
[3] [1987] AC 625.
[4] [1994] AC 531.

The basic principles which make up the doctrine of procedural fairness can broadly be stated as follows:

- The person affected by a decision should receive notice of the decision being made against him/her.[5]
- The decision-maker should make adequate disclosure to the person to be affected by the decision of information held against him/her, and the person to be affected by the decision should have the opportunity to make representations.[6]
- The decision-maker should not be biased.[7]
- The decision-maker should give reasons for the decision made.

A particular word should be offered at this point about this last principle, the requirement of reasons. The courts have consistently stressed that there is no absolute and general obligation at common law to give reasons for decisions.[8] However, this is not to say that reasons are never required as a matter of law. Increasingly, the courts are prepared to impose the obligation, particularly where a lack of reasons contributes to a lack of fairness.[9] The requirement of giving reasons for decisions sits comfortably under the heading of procedural fairness and is best thought of as an inherent principle of administrative law due to the fact that, consistent with the other principles which make up the doctrine of procedural fairness, it is a flexible principle which requires application in context. As Sedley J observed in *R v Higher Education Funding Council ex parte the Institute of Dental Surgery*,[10]

> each case will come to rest between two poles, or possibly at one of them: the decision which cries out for reasons, and the decision for which reasons are entirely inapposite. Somewhere between the two poles comes the dividing line separating those cases in which the balance of factors calls for reasons from those where it does not.

[5] *Ridge v Baldwin* [1964] AC 40; *R v Secretary of State for the Home Department Ex p Al-Fayed (No 1)* [1998] 1 WLR 763.

[6] *Board of Education v Rice* [1911] AC 179; *Inland Revenue Comrs v Hood Barrs* 1961 SC (HL) 22; *Kanda v Malaya* [1962] AC 322; *Attorney General v Ryan* [1980] AC 718.

[7] *R v Leicestershire Fire Authority ex parte Thompson* (1978) 77 LGR 373; *R v Secretary of State for the Environment ex parte Kirkstall Valley Campaign Ltd* [1996] 3 All ER 304.

[8] *R v Home Secretary ex parte Doody* [1994] 1 AC 531; *R v Minister of Defence ex parte Murray* [1998] COD 134.

[9] *R v Civil Services Appeal Board ex parte Cunningham* [1991] 4 All ER 310; *R v Home Secretary ex parte Doody* [1994] 1 AC 531; *R v Higher Education Funding Council ex parte the Institute of Dental Surgery* [1994] 1 All ER 651.

[10] [1994] 1 All ER 651 at 666.

The essence of procedural fairness is that its principles can be, and indeed must be, applied with varying degrees of intensity according to what the context requires.[11] So, for example, the requirement of prior notice may not actually involve informing every last person who might be affected by a decision so long as reasonable steps have been taken to alert those affected,[12] though if an individual is likely to suffer particular loss as a result of a proposed decision, the duty to ensure notification will be applied more strictly.[13] Similarly, the right to make representations may be as limited as the opportunity to write to the administrative body on the basis of having received notice of a proposed decision,[14] or may require the ability to make oral representations to a hearing.[15] As Lord Gill noted in *Young v Criminal Injuries Compensation Board*,[16] there is a difference 'between a right to a hearing and a right to be heard'. And as we have already seen above, the requirement of reasons is also variably applied.

What is of particular interest for our purposes here is to examine the circumstances under which the principles of procedural fairness are applied minimally and to note the justifications for this. By looking at the situations where the intensity of application of the principles is low (or where they need not be respected at all) we can discover the competing concerns which justify this low intensity of application and begin to tease out competing models of procedural fairness. There appear to be two principal justifications for a low intensity of application: (1) the need for administrative efficiency; and (2) the protection of national security. Both of these points can be illustrated briefly and quite straightforwardly.

Administrative Efficiency

The courts have long had a interest in promoting (or at least in not interfering with) the efficient workings of government agencies.

---

[11] *Board of Education v Rice* [1911] AC 179.
[12] *Wilson v Secretary of State for Environment* [1973] 1 WLR 1083.
[13] *R v Secretary of State for Health, ex p US Tobacco International Inc* [1992] QB 353.
[14] *R v Housing Appeal Tribunal* [1920] 3 KB 334.
[15] *Lloyd v McMahon* [1987] AC 625.
[16] 1997 SLT 297.

Indeed, the pre-*Ridge v Baldwin*[17] distinction between judicial and administrative functions[18] served to protect the administration from undue interference which would militate against efficient government administration.[19] In the contemporary context, the House of Lords has recently re-emphasised its concern with administrative efficiency in interpreting the requirements of Article 6(1) of the European Convention on Human Rights in relation to the administration of homelessness law. In *Begum v London Borough of Tower Hamlets*[20] a challenge was made to the statutory system of internal administrative review followed by an appeal on a point of law to the county court[21] on the ground that it contravened Article 6(1) of the European Convention on Human Rights—the requirement that civil rights and obligations be determined in a fair hearing by an independent and impartial tribunal. The challenge was resolved around the issue of whether the county court enjoyed 'full jurisdiction'. The House ruled that it did, following its previous decision in the Alconbury case[22] that 'full jurisdiction' did not mean review on both merits and law—full decision-making power—but rather meant 'full jurisdiction to deal with the case as the nature of the decision requires'.[23] The House focused on the potential adverse impact of a contrary decision on the operations of the homelessness legislation. As Lord Bingham phrased it, there was a concern to avoid the 'emasculation' of welfare administration through over-judicialisation.

In such cases,[24] the courts recognise the tension that exists between bureaucratic efficiency and a high-intensity application of the principles of procedural fairness. The more the application of the principles of procedural fairness approximate trial-type procedural protections, the greater the burden is on the routine workings of the administrative system. It is not hard to see, then, two competing models of procedural

---

[17] [1964] AC 40.

[18] For example, *Local Government Board v Arlidge* [1915] AC 120; *Errington v Minister of Health* [1935] 1 KB 249.

[19] *Local Government Board v Arlidge* [1915] AC 120.

[20] [2003] 2 WLR 388.

[21] Housing Act 1996, Part VII.

[22] *R (on the Application of Alconbury Developments Ltd) v Secretary of State for Environment, Transport and the Regions* [2001] HRLR 45.

[23] per Lord Hoffman at para 87.

[24] See also, for example, *Wiseman v Borneman* [1971] AC 297.

fairness emerge from the case law. Both represent end-points of a continuum and are separated by a spectrum of application.[25] The first model is where administrative efficiency is privileged and the principles of procedural fairness are applied, accordingly, with low intensity. The second is where the desire for administrative efficiency is trumped by the interests of the citizen(s) and where the principles of procedural fairness are, accordingly, applied with high intensity. This model approximates trial-type protections and can be characterised as 'adjudicative fairness'. Although these models and the spectrum between them may be 'sown in an adjudicative framework' (Craig, 2003: 452), there is still sufficient difference between them for it to be meaningful to talk in terms of competing models. It is also not difficult to see that these models resemble some of those developed in the theoretical literature discussed above. The opposing doctrinal models of procedural fairness approximate Mashaw's models of bureaucratic rationality and moral judgment. They are perhaps even closer to Galligan's models of 'bureaucratic administration' and 'fair treatment' (1996: 237–40). This means, then, that Adler (with Longhurst 1994; with Henman 2001) is mistaken in describing Mashaw's moral judgment model as the 'legality model' and setting it against the bureaucratic rationality model. The reality is that both the moral judgment model and the bureaucratic rationality model are reflected in administrative law doctrine, and so *both* may be described as falling within 'legality'.

National Security

The second justification for applying the principles of procedural fairness with low intensity, or not applying them at all, is in the interests of protecting national security. The *GCHQ* case[26] provides a clear example of this. Here the issue was whether the employees' union should have been consulted about a decision to prohibit union membership and thereby be given an opportunity of making representations to the minister prior to the decision. The ban on union membership was

---

[25] For a discussion of the considerations applied in determining at which point along the continuum the context lies, see Craig (2003: 425–31).

[26] *Council for Civil Service Unions v Minister for the Civil Service* [1985] AC 374.

framed in terms of protecting national security. In the House of Lords, the minister argued that the failure to consult and to allow representations was similarly justified in the interests of national security—that consultation about the proposed decision may have prompted the very strike action which the proposal was intended to avoid. This argument was accepted by the House.

Relative to the 'administrative efficiency' justification, a 'national security' justification for the low application of procedural fairness principles is perhaps reasonably uncommon in practice.[27] However, it is certainly well-established in law. The message conveyed to the administration in such situations is the same as that of the administrative efficiency model—that the principles of procedural fairness may be minimally applied or not applied at all.

RATIONALITY OF DECISION-MAKING PROCESS

Although procedural fairness represents the classic case of the flexibility of administrative law doctrine, there is also considerable room for manoeuvre within the doctrines relating to the rationality of decision-making processes. Certain of the administrative law principles regarding the rationality of decisions also play out the tension between individual and agency interests. Two of the principles are considered in this section. They are as follows:

- The decision-maker should not fetter his/her discretion by the adoption of rigid policies, but must consider each case on its merits.
- The decision-maker should consider all relevant facts and exclude from consideration all irrelevant facts.

Administrative Policies

The first principle—that decision-makers should not adopt overly-rigid policies—is an application within administrative law of the more general principle that the exercise of discretion requires attention to the particularities of a case. The discretion exercised by the court in its

---

[27] For other examples, see *R v Secretary of State for the Home Department ex parte Hosenball* [1977] 3 All ER 452; *R v Secretary of State for the Home Department ex parte Cheblak* [1991] 2 All ER 319.

adjudicative functions provides the paradigmatic example of this principle. As Lord President Clyde noted in *McCallum v Arthur*,[28] 'a discretion necessarily connotes a consideration of individual circumstances, not a formulation or application of general principles.' However, within the field of administrative law, this principle is modified to the extent that the adoption of policies is acceptable so long as the decision-maker is willing to consider deviations from policy which are required by the particular circumstances of individual cases.[29] In applying this principle, the courts have at times promoted a model of decision-making which approximates (in a weak form) the use of discretion in court adjudication. Here, policies are tolerated, but only as one relevant consideration among many.[30] The infringement of policies on the exercise of discretion is, accordingly, minimised. However, the stronger line of authority appears to be that policies may set up a presumption of how a decision should be made, but cannot be completely determinative. Decision-makers must be open to exceptional cases. In the classic statement on the matter, Bankes LJ drew a distinction between two administrative practices in relation to policy, where only the first is lawful:

> There are on the one hand cases where a tribunal in honest exercise of its discretion has adopted a policy, and, without refusing to hear an applicant, intimates to him what its policy is, and that after hearing him it will in accordance with its policy decide against him, unless there is something exceptional in its case . . . On the other hand there are cases where a tribunal has passed a rule, or come to a determination, not to hear any application of a particular character by whomsoever made.[31]

However, even within this more permissive line of authority,[32] the courts have applied this principle with varying degrees of intensity, showing at times considerable reluctance to interfere with the agency's

[28] 1955 SC 188 at 197.

[29] *R v London County Council ex parte Corrie* [1918] 1 KB 68; *R v Port of London Authority ex parte Kynoch Ltd* [1919] 1 KB 176; *Kilmarnock Magistrates v Secretary of State for Scotland* 1961 SC 350.

[30] *Stringer v Minister of Housing and Local Government* [1970] 1 WLR 1281; *H Lavender & Sons v Minister of Housing and Local Government* [1970] 1 WLR 1231; *R v Rotherham Licensing JJ ex parte Chapman* [1939] 2 All ER 710. These cases are discussed fully in Galligan (1976).

[31] *R v Port of London Authority ex parte Kynoch Ltd* [1919] 1 KB 176.

[32] For examples of where the court has interfered with decisions for an over-rigid application of policy, see *Attorney General ex rel Tilley v Wandsworth LBC* [1981] 1 WLR 854; *Elliott v Brighton BC* (1980) 79 LGR 506; *R v Secretary of State for the Environment ex parte Hatton BC* (1983) LGR 662.

use of policy. Like procedural fairness, the competition here is between the interests of the agency and those of the citizen. Galligan puts it succinctly when he notes:

> The central issue in the legal control of policies is now clear: it is the resolution of the apparent conflict between the interest of the decision-maker in developing policies which determine particular decisions and the interest of the individual in obtaining discretionary decisions which take proper account of the special features of his claim. (1976: 335)

The courts have recognised the importance of policies to efficient administrative practice and have used this to apply the principle very minimally. For example, in *British Oxygen Co Ltd v Board of Trade*[33] the House of Lords considered a challenge to a departmental policy that investment grants should not be given in relation to applications involving items costing less than £25. British Oxygen Co Ltd applied for and were refused funding in relation to its £4m investment in oxygen cylinders, each of which cost approximately £20. It sought judicial review of this refusal, arguing that the minister had unlawfully fettered his discretion. The House of Lords disagreed. Lord Reid observed,

> the circumstances in which discretions are exercised vary enormously and [the dictum of Bankes LJ in the *Kynoch* case] cannot be applied literally in every case. The general rule is that anyone who has to exercise a discretion must not 'shut his ears to an application' . . . But a Ministry or large authority may have had to deal already with a multitude of similar applications and then they will almost certainly have evolved a policy so precise that it could well be called a rule. There can be no objections to that, provided the authority is always willing to listen to anyone with something new to say.

Viscount Dilhorne gave more explicit guidance on the extent of the requirement not to 'shut one's ears' to an application:

> It was both reasonable and right that the Board should make known to those interested the policy it was going to follow. By doing so fruitless applications involving expense and expenditure of time might be avoided . . . I must confess that I feel some doubt whether the words used by Bankes LJ . . . are really applicable to a case of this kind. It seems somewhat pointless and a waste of time that the Board should have to consider applications which are bound as a result of its policy decision to fail.

Although the principle controlling the use of administrative policy does not share the explicit and structured flexibility of procedural

---

[33] [1971] AC 610.

fairness, we can nevertheless see a variation in how it is applied by the court. On the one hand, the courts privilege the interests of the agency in promoting administrative efficiency and apply the principle with low intensity. At the other end of the spectrum, the courts privilege the interests of the individual, imposing stricter standards and being more willing to interfere with the use of policy, even to the extent of treating it as only one relevant consideration among many in the decision-making process. Like procedural fairness, then, we can see the emergence of the same two models of administrative justice at opposite ends of a continuum. The same competition can be found in relation to the doctrine of relevant facts.

Relevant and Irrelevant Facts

Within the terminology of administrative law, the principle concerned with relevancy can be subsumed under a heading of 'reasonableness'.[34] It may be also be regarded as being an instance of the requirement of public authorities to act within the powers granted by Parliament, particularly where the decision-maker has failed to take account of matters which the statute expressly requires the decision-making to think about. Clyde and Edwards discuss it under the heading of 'Error' (2000: 608). The relevancy principle also easily bleeds into the principle against using public powers for improper purposes[35] and can additionally be framed in terms of decision-makers asking the wrong question and so misdirecting themselves in law.[36] However, for our purposes it is more helpful, it is suggested, to think about it as relating to the rationality of decisions—in the common understanding of this word. In seeking to ensure that administrative decision-makers consider all relevant facts and exclude from consideration irrelevant facts, administrative law is policing the rationality of the decision-making process—the connection between the decision-outcome and the cognitive process of getting there. When making a decision, it is irrational to take into account irrelevant matters, or to disregard relevant matters (Airo-Farulla, 2001). To do so unsettles the basis of the decision.

---

[34] *Associated Provincial Picture Houses Ltd v Wednesbury Corporation* [1948] 1 KB 223.

[35] See, for example, *R v East Sussex County Court ex parte Tandy* [1998] AC 714.

[36] See, for example, *Wilson v Nithsdale* SLT 1992 113.

The question of what is and is not relevant to a government decision is a matter for the courts. The ability of the courts to scrutinise the reasoning behind decisions and to test the various factors considered for relevancy is very broad and applies even where the government has been granted a wide discretion to take action when it considers it appropriate.[37] The weight given by decision-makers to particular relevant factors is usually treated as a matter for the public body concerned (unless the weight given is so absurd that no reasonable decision-maker would have done the same),[38] though the courts have at times gone further and quashed decisions because the decision-maker relied too heavily on one relevant factor.[39]

The aspect of this principle which is important for our purposes relates to the case law concerning the relevance of financial resources to decision-making. The case law expresses some ambivalence within which we can see the familiar tension between the demands of administrative expediency and the interests of the individual who is the subject of the decision in question. The cases which have considered the relevance of financial resources wrestle with the basic competition inherent in government administration between individual and collective interests.[40] In *R v Gloucestershire County Council ex parte Barry*[41] the House of Lords had to consider a council's decision about how to fulfil its duty to an individual who was elderly and disabled. His needs had been assessed by a council social worker under the Chronically Sick and Disabled Persons Act 1970. The council were under a duty to meet these needs. According to the assessment, he needed home care for shopping, a pension, laundry and cleaning, and meals on wheels. However, he was later informed that the council could no longer provide laundry and cleaning because of a reduction in funding. Mr Barry challenged this decision, asserting that the council was wrong to

[37] *Padfield v Minister of Agriculture, Fisheries and Food* [1968] AC 997.

[38] *Tesco Stores Ltd v Secretary of State for the Environment* [1995] 1 WLR 759; *London and Midland Developments v Secretary of State for Scotland* 1996 SCLR 465.

[39] *South Oxfordshire District Council v Secretary of State for the Environment* [1981] 1 WLR 1092.

[40] See, for example, the judgment of Lord Cooke in *R v Chief Constable of Sussex ex parte International Trader's Ferry Ltd* [1999] 2 AC 418 concerning the decision of the Chief Constable during a period of public protesting to restrict on financial grounds the policing of a port, and hence commercial ferry traffic, to two days a week. Lord Cooke observed: 'the case can equally be seen as a conflict, not between the company and the lawbreakers but between the policing needs of the company and those of all the rest of the public of Sussex.'

[41] [1997] AC 584.

consider its financial capabilities in deciding how to fulfil its duty to meet his needs. The House of Lords was divided. The majority, however, held that in interpreting 'needs' it was necessary for the council to take account of its financial capabilities. Lord Nicholls observed (at pp 604 and 605),

> needs for services cannot sensibly be assessed without having some regard to the cost of providing them. A person's need for a particular type or level of service cannot be decided in a vacuum from which all considerations of cost have been expelled . . . Once it is accepted, as surely must be right, that cost is a relevant factor in assessing a person's needs for the services listed in section 2(1), then in deciding how much weight is to be attached to cost some evaluation or assumption has to be made about the impact which the cost will have upon the authority. Cost is of more or less significance depending upon whether the authority currently has more or less money. Thus, depending upon the authority's financial position, so the eligibility criteria, setting out the degree of disability which must exist before help will be provided with laundry or cleaning or whatever, may properly be more or less stringent.

In a later case, however,[42] the House of Lords took a different line. It had to consider the decision of a local education authority to reduce the quantity of home education given to a child with special needs following a cut in central government funding. The education authority were under a duty to arrange suitable education according to the pupil's educational needs. The question was whether the authority had erred in also taking account of its broader financial position. The House ruled that it had. Lord Browne-Wilkinson noted (at p 749):

> To permit a local authority to avoid performing a statutory duty on the grounds that it prefers to spend the money in other ways is to downgrade a statutory duty to a discretionary power . . . If Parliament wishes to reduce public expenditure on meeting the needs of sick children then it is up to Parliament so to provide.

The courts then, even in cases such as these where a duty is involved,[43] are capable of giving different signals to government about the relevance of financial resources to decision-making. The area of administration under scrutiny seems to be important. It is perhaps

[42] *R v East Sussex County Court ex parte Tandy* [1998] AC 714.
[43] See also *R v Chief Constable of Sussex ex parte International Trader's Ferry Ltd* [1999] 2 AC 418. Consideration of resources has been held to be relevant where the public authority has a discretion to exercise, as opposed to a duty to fulfil. See, for example, *R v Cambridge Health Authority ex parte B* [1995] 1 WLR 898.

significant that, in distinguishing *Barry*, Lord Browne-Wilkinson in
Tandy noted that

> the statutory provision . . . under consideration [in *Barry*] was a strange one.
> The statutory duty was to arrange certain benefits to meet the 'needs' of the
> disabled persons but the lack of certain of the benefits enumerated in the
> section could not possibly give rise to 'need' in any stringent sense of the
> word. Thus it is difficult to talk about the lack of a radio or a holiday or a
> recreational activity as giving rise to a need: they may be desirable but they
> are not in any ordinary sense necessities. Yet, according to the section the
> disabled person's needs were to be capable of being met by the provision of
> such benefits.

In designing policies and in routine decision-making there is usually
(perhaps always) a competition for the administrator between the
interests of the agency (in terms of administrative efficiency) and the
interests of the individual (in this case in terms of substantive benefit).
This competition is a practical problem which must be attended to by
the agency concerned. The case law described above, offers varying
guidance to public agencies about the extent to which they may sacri-
fice the individual's interest for the sake of administrative efficiency.
Once again we can see the courts offering competing images according
to context of whose interests should be privileged.

CONCLUSION TO PART 4

This chapter has attempted to set out and justify the final hypothesis of
the book regarding the conditions which must exist to maximise judicial review's effectiveness in securing compliance with administrative
law. The hypothesis is that for compliance to be secured, judicial
review must project a consistent image of administrative justice in
relation to particular areas of government decision-making—or at
least to develop the image of administrative justice sufficiently slowly
that public bodies do not become confused and are able to keep track.

As we noted in chapter 6, there is an obvious sense in which it is true
that if courts hope to have any impact on respondent bodies they
should be consistent in their decision-making. So, where, for example
the limits of a public body's legal mandate is set out in judicial review,
or where the precise meaning of a legal term or concept is given, the
courts (at least of the same or lower levels) should not contradict themselves. This much is clear and underpins the notion of precedent.

However, the argument of this part of the book goes deeper. Judicial review, as noted in chapter 1, can perform a number of functions. It acts as an individual dispute resolution mechanism. Additionally, it may clarify the interpretation of legal terms or concepts. However, for the purposes of this part, the important function of judicial review is that it conveys messages to public bodies about how they should fashion and go about their decision-making activities. This function reaches beyond the individual dispute or the meaning of legal terms. It embodies the regulatory capacity of judicial review. The central argument here is that within administrative law doctrine, just as in the socio-legal literature, we can find a plurality of images of administrative justice. I have set out two basic competitions that are inherent in administrative law: first, the competition between the interests of the agency in implementing law on the one hand, and the interests of the individual as the subject of that implementation process on the other; secondly, there is the competition between judicial control and agency autonomy about who gets to decide what. The implications of these competitions for compliance are that when decision-makers reflect upon particular decision-making tasks and seek to understand the guidance from the courts about (1) how they should interact with the citizen, and (2) how much leeway they have to trust their own expertise and judgment, the courts must answer consistently.

It is not claimed that all matters which fall within the province of administrative law can be explained in terms of these twin competitions. That would be too bold a claim. However, it *is* claimed that these two competitions go the heart of administrative law, and are sufficiently central to its enterprise that it renders the meaning of administrative law contingent for respondent bodies. Under the 'agency interest' model, bureaucratic efficiency is privileged at the expense of the procedural protections enjoyed by the individual citizen. Under the 'individual interest' model, on the other hand, the individual is the focus of the development of administrative practices, at the expense of bureaucratic efficiency. These two models clearly approximate the models of procedural justice discussed in the work of Mashaw (1983) and Galligan (1996).

Under the agency autonomy model of decision-making, public bodies enjoy wide discretion in fashioning their decision-making processes and in the substance of their decision-making outcomes. They are permitted to follow their preferences, exercise their expertise and trust their judgment, secure in the knowledge that the courts are holding back from interfering too much. Under the judicial control model, however, the courts show much greater willingness to exercise control and to substitute their preferences for those of the public body. This requires the public body to discover the courts' preferences on pertinent issues and to take the lead from them. These models are not matched by comparable discussion in the socio-legal literature, though one might see some links between the role of expertise in the 'agency autonomy' model and Mashaw's professional treatment model and in Kagan's (1978) expertise model of regulatory justice.

Both sets of models represent end points on a continuum and I have attempted to illustrate how the various doctrines of administrative law retain sufficient flexibility so that they can be used by the courts to promote opposing models within each competition. It should be noted that certain doctrines lend themselves to broader spectrums. The doctrines of procedural fairness, for example, arguably have a broader spectrum when compared with the doctrine of *Wednesbury* unreasonableness. Nevertheless, taken generally, the competitions are observable and the opposing models sufficiently distinct that the requirement of consistency is brought to the fore and worthy of particular attention.

Of course, as a final observation, it is recognised that one might easily take issue with the models of administrative justice set out in this part of the book. However, it is important to note that whether or not one agrees with the precise form of the models outlined here is to an extent beside the point (though I hope to have persuaded some). What matters more is the assertion that the messages which emanate from judicial review about how to fashion and go about the decision-making process are various and so contingent. If this point is taken, then it does not matter if one wishes to challenge the identity of the models above. For judicial review to secure compliance with administrative law, it must still project consistent images of administrative justice in relation to particular areas of administrative decision-making.

Part 5: Conclusion

9

Judicial Review and Compliance with Administrative Law

INTRODUCTION

ASSESSING THE IMPACT of judicial review on administrative decision-making has now become an important concern for administrative law scholarship in the UK—and rightly so. Judicial decision-making seems to rest at times upon assumptions about the practical effects of the courts' rulings (Richardson and Sunkin, 1996; Harlow and Rawlings, 1997: 566), and knowledge about the empirical relationship between judicial review and government administration may also prove important for legal practitioners (Sunkin, 2004). Any attempts to reform or influence government administration through administrative law calls for empirical enquiry to test the effects of such efforts (Coglianese, 2002). More significantly, however, the study of administrative law would be severely impoverished by a failure to explore the range of responses of government administration to judicial scrutiny. Notions such as the rule of law are powerful normative claims in democratic states and set up an agenda for empirical research. Judicial mandates for bureaucratic behaviour have an authoritative and prescriptive quality which unavoidably invite social enquiry. If the courts set out some level of guidance about how government should go about its business, it is difficult to resist the temptation to at least try to find out if and how law matters—regardless of how difficult the task is, or how elusive the answers might be (Hertogh and Halliday, 2004). After a number of calls for empirical enquiry to this end (see, for example, Rawlings, 1986; Cranston, 1994; Galligan, 1996), socio-legal scholars have responded and a small number of studies have emerged in recent years (summarised in Richardson, 2004).

The aim of this book has been to complement this emerging body of work and to inform future enquiry. The case studies of homelessness decision-making have given deeper insights into the barriers to judicial review's influence and have exposed some of its limitations as an enforcement mechanism. Furthermore, the approach of this book has been to use this empirical study of administrative decision-making in heavily litigated government agencies to develop an analytical framework which can help us think more generally about the effectiveness of judicial review in securing compliance with administrative law. Research on the impact of judicial review to date would suggest that the influence of judicial review on administrative decision-making is patchy and varied. The development of an analytical framework may not only assist us in speculating about whether and to what extent judicial review might be influential in a given administrative context, it may also help us explain the patchy impact of judicial review in the areas of administration which have been investigated and to detect some pattern or form in the seemingly random impact of judicial review generally. The framework lays a foundation for our understanding of the dynamic relationship between judicial and administrative decision-making. The series of hypotheses can be carefully tested in a range of administrative settings, and our knowledge of the influence of judicial review can slowly be deepened and refined. The job of exploring the relationship between judicial and administrative decision-making is still in its infancy and much work requires to be done to build up a more comprehensive and reliable picture of the significance of the courts to government administration. It is hoped that the thesis of this book will be helpful to this task.

The aim of this concluding chapter is to draw together the strands of the overall thesis. In its remainder I address three issues. First, I summarise the analytical approach and framework of the book, offering an informed snapshot of the basic thesis of the study. Secondly, I address the question of whether the framework is applicable beyond the confines of the case study—the administration of homelessness law. And thirdly, the book concludes with a brief consideration of the potential direction of future research.

THE ANALYTICAL APPROACH OF THIS BOOK

Typologies of Decision-Makers

Regulation scholars have enhanced our understanding of regulatory compliance by developing typologies of regulatees. Most famous, perhaps, is Kagan and Scholz's 'criminology of the corporation' (1984) (though see also Baldwin, 1995; and Kagan, Gunningham and Thornton, 2003). Kagan and Scholz stress the point that regulatees are not a homogenous group, but are diverse in their abilities and propensities to comply with regulation. They illustrate this point by developing a typology of corporations as follows:

- *Amoral calculators* Such corporations are classically 'bad apples'. They are profit-oriented, disrespectful and apathetic about law. Non-compliance stems from economic calculation.
- *Political citizens* These corporations are ordinarily inclined to obey the law. Their commitment, however, is contingent on principled agreement with the law or regulation as not being unreasonable or arbitrary.
- *Incompetent organisations* Such firms are inclined to obey the law but commit violations due to organisational failure: the failure to oversee, to calculate intelligently or to establish mechanisms that keep all actors aware of, and attentive to the developing content of law and regulation.

Typologies such as these are very useful in highlighting and describing the diversity of the regulated population. And, of course, typologies of government agencies would be equally possible to construct. They would similarly shed light on the fact that individual agencies or sub-sections of agencies—or even teams within sub-sections—will differ from each other in many important respects. Just as the corporate population is not homogenous, so the government population is not homogenous. However, within (or underlying) these typologies lie the attributes of the corporations which impact upon the extent of their compliance, and this, it is suggested, is the most significant contribution of such typologies to our understanding of compliance. By examining the typologies we can discover the factors which make a difference to (non-)compliant behaviour. The approach of this book has been to separate out and focus directly upon these factors. Despite the illuminating qualities of typologies, they run the risk of being interpreted too rigidly, and thereby of betraying the range and subtlety of diversity within the regulated population which is not necessarily captured by the ideal types. We should attempt, where possible, to seek out these subtle differences which exist in social reality between regulatees (and which can be observed in relation to single regulatees over time). The analytical approach of this book is designed to help us do this.

Continuums of Conditions Affecting Compliance

One of the main claims of this book, as already noted, is that the conditions outlined which impact upon judicial review's effectiveness in securing compliance with administrative law should be viewed in terms of the degree to which they are satisfied, rather than whether or not they are satisfied. The conditions represent continuums along which individual agencies may be situated (and along which they shift over time). A very fluid picture of compliance behaviour, then, is built up where subtleties can be appreciated and observed because of the explicit focus on the features of the administrative realm which condition the responses to administrative law's regulation. Additionally, of course, the analysis of this book focuses not just on the internal dynamics and attributes of the government agencies, but also looks at the decision-making environment and the law itself. In relation to these elements too, we saw that continuums exist which condition judicial review's effectiveness in securing compliance. Not every continuum has the same breadth of scope, but the continuums exist nevertheless. In relation to the decision-making environment, the continuum spans the extent to which law is in competition with alternative normative forces, and the extent to which the environment is conducive to the strength of law as a normative force. In relation to the law, we saw that the common law is inherently uncertain about what compliance with administrative law requires, thereby placing particular emphasis on the condition that the law must project clear and consistent messages about what the law requires in relation to particular kinds of decision-making. The extent to which the courts do this in judicial review is one of the determinants of its effectiveness. The basic arguments about these continuums are summarised below.

The Decision-Makers

In relation to the decision-makers we set out three conditions. The first related to the reception of legal knowledge into administrative agencies and this was discussed in chapter 2. Here we focused on the extent to which all those with an input into decision-making know what the law requires of them in exercising their discretion. At one end of the continuum, then, we have a low level of knowledge, and at the other we have a high level of knowledge. The second condition, explored in chapter 3, concerned legal conscientiousness. At one end of the continuum we have a low level of legal conscientiousness where decision-makers do not care about law and engage in practices of creative compliance to avoid legal control, or flagrantly disobey legal requirements. Conscientious compliance is at other end of the spectrum. Here decision-makers have a commitment to legality and seek to conscientiously comply in all their decision-making. The final condition in relation to the decision-makers was discussed in chapter 4 and concerned their legal competence. At the low end of the continuum decision-makers apply legal knowledge by developing narrow rules and apply their legal knowledge only to the decision-making task which has been scrutinised in judicial review. At the high end of the continuum, decision-makers derive general principles from judicial review decisions and apply them widely to all relevant decision-making tasks within their remit.

The Decision-Making Environment

Chapter 5 discussed the decision-making environment. Here the continuum relates to the extent to which there is a convergence between the demands of law and the demands of alternative normative systems. However, given that some level competition is the norm, the continuum also relates to the strength of law within the environment, and this concern is perhaps more pertinent for our understanding of the influence of judicial review. At the low end of the spectrum, law is a weak normative force within the decision-making environment and is routinely trumped by other normative demands. At the high end of the spectrum, law is the dominant influence, or normative demands have converged and there is no competition at all.

The Law

The final element of the administrative realm, as we saw in chapters 6, 7 and 8, concerned the law. Some aspects of what I have described as 'administrative law'—for example, the development or refinement of statutory concepts, or clarification of statutory duties—are fairly straightforward and the condition here is that the courts are clear and consistent in their rulings. However, in many aspects of administrative law—particularly the application of the common law principles—we saw that the law is inherently undecided about what it requires of different decision-makers. Administrative justice is not only contested in the socio-legal literature, it is also contested in legal doctrine and we can see some (though not complete) correspondence between models of administrative justice in the socio-legal literature, and models of administrative justice in legal doctrine. The question of what compliance with administrative law requires has a number of legal answers. This makes the possibility that the law fails to be clear or consistent all the more likely, and broadens, it is suggested, the corresponding spectrum. At the low end, the courts apply the law in an unclear and inconsistent fashion and the law, therefore, is confusing for decision-makers who conscientiously seek to apply it. At the high end of the spectrum, the courts apply administrative law clearly and consistently and there no room for confusion.

This analytical framework can be further summarised in the diagram opposite.

APPLYING THE FRAMEWORK BEYOND THE CONTEXT
OF HOMELESSNESS ADMINISTRATION

Introduction

The framework of this book, summarised in the above section, has been built out of an empirical study of the administration of homelessness law in local government. To many scholars of public law this will seem like a peculiar, remote and unrepresentative corner of public administration. In many ways it is. In thinking about the significance of judicial review to government decision-making, then, important and legitimate questions may be asked about how widely we can apply the lessons learned through a study of homelessness administration to other areas of government. As Sunkin has noted (2004), organisational context is important to the study of judicial review's impact. Homelessness administration is a context 'where we might expect law and legal values to be distant and the likely impact of judicial review remote.'

Representativeness, of course, is a fundamental problem for social science research. But it is less of an issue, it is suggested, for the development of an analytical framework such as the one set out in this book. This is for two reasons. First, as we noted above, the framework is comprised of a set of conditions which represent continuums. It has

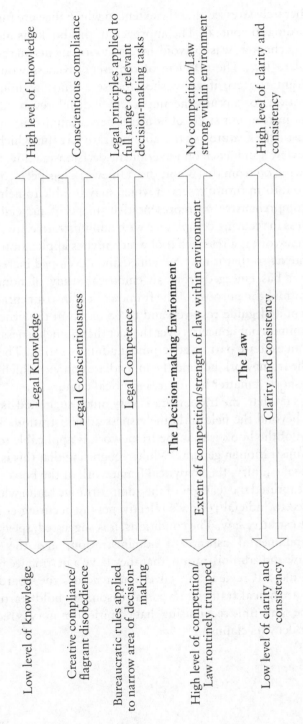

The Decision-makers

High level of knowledge ⟸ Legal Knowledge ⟹ Low level of knowledge

Conscientious compliance ⟸ Legal Conscientiousness ⟹ Creative compliance/ flagrant disobedience

Legal principles applied to full range of relevant decision-making tasks ⟸ Legal Competence ⟹ Bureaucratic rules applied to narrow area of decision-making

The Decision-making Environment

No competition/Law strong within environment ⟸ Extent of competition/strength of law within environment ⟹ High level of competition/ Law routinely trumped

The Law

High level of clarity and consistency ⟸ Clarity and consistency ⟹ Low level of clarity and consistency

Fig 1. *Summary of analytical framework*

been deliberately stressed that the extent to which they are fulfilled will vary according to context. The approach of this book, as indicated in the opening chapter, was to avoid any pronouncements on the 'impact' of judicial review. The problem of representativeness would indeed be a relevant concern if we wished to use a study of homelessness administration to capture the impact of judicial review across the board. But instead our study of homelessness administration has been used to distil the features of the administrative realm which mediate judicial review's influence on government decision-making. Secondly, and following on from this point, the framework has been constructed in order to inform future research which may be able to help us build a more comprehensive or representative image of judicial review's effectiveness in securing compliance with administrative law. The analytical framework is a research tool which invites application in a variety of contexts so that it may be refined and developed incrementally. Although it has emerged from an empirical study of homelessness administration, the purpose of the framework is instrumental. Its goal is to inform and guide research and to be tested in the process. This should minimise our concerns over the fact that homelessness administration is an esoteric part of government administration. The applicability of the framework beyond the immediate context which gave rise to it is, in short, a matter for future empirical enquiry.

Having said that, the framework is very much suggested as having a relevance beyond the field of homelessness administration. The basic contention of the book is that the framework is applicable to government administration in general. While recognising that this is a matter for empirical enquiry, the analytical framework of the book is offered as having captured the features of the administrative realm which make a difference to judicial review's effectiveness in securing compliance with administrative law. The conditions, it is suggested, speak to sufficiently fundamental aspects of administration, and the interface between law and administration, that they have a pertinence for thinking about judicial review and government across the board. In this sense, the analytical framework has a reasonably bold starting point while at the same time recognising that empirical enquiry is required to confirm or deny its claims.

Varying Significance of Legal Conscientiousness According to Context

Nevertheless, despite the above defence about the applicability of the analytical framework beyond the field of homelessness administration, there are some important observations that we can make at this stage which highlight a limitation of the framework (though it is also useful in raising new research questions and so guiding future research). There is a limited sense in which it is important to be aware of a lack of representativeness in interpreting and applying the analytical framework. The data which gave rise to the framework implicitly made suggestions about the level of importance of legal conscientiousness to judicial review's capacity to secure compliance with administrative law. This was not done in any precise way and the analysis deliberately avoided making specific claims about the significance of the conditions, relative to each other, to compliance with administrative law. However, in reading the empirical data in this study, one inevitably gains a general sense of how significant legal conscientiousness was to judicial review's effectiveness in the context of homelessness administration. Such a general sense, however, should not necessarily be translated to other contexts. Another way of thinking about this is to note that a lower level of legal conscientiousness may not be such a problem for judicial review's influence in other decision-making contexts. This is a separate point from the one made above that we should expect to see the conditions fulfilled to different extents in different contexts. The point here is that legal conscientiousness may not need to be fulfilled to the same extent in different contexts for judicial review's capacity as a regulator to be maximised. In other words, judicial review may do just as good a job in securing compliance with administrative law in other contexts despite the fact that the condition of legal conscientiousness is fulfilled to lesser extent when compared with homelessness administration. Some further explanation of this is required.

Legal Conscientiousness and Homelessness Administration

In chapter 3, I examined the concept of legal conscientiousness and argued that one of the conditions for the maximisation of judicial review's effectiveness in securing compliance with administrative law was that decision-makers must have a commitment to legality and must care about acting lawfully. However, legitimate questions might be asked about how important legal conscientiousness is to full compliance with administrative law. Surely, it might be argued, an inner commitment to the values of law is not required so long as the principles of law are applied and the rules followed in one's decision-making tasks? Surely compliance with the law could be achieved by cynics? To an extent this is true. The contention of this section is that the role of legal conscientiousness in promoting compliance with administrative law will vary according to context.

Certainly in relation to the administration of homelessness law, the data from this study demonstrated that legal conscientiousness was an important requirement for the maximisation of compliance. There are three factors which justified the treatment of legal conscientiousness in chapter 3. First is the role of sanctions in judicial review, second is the number of administrative decisions made relative to the incidence of judicial review, and third is the complexity of organisations and the diffusion of discretion within them.

The Role of Sanctions

In chapter 5 we looked at the extent to which judicial review may operate as a sanction. In relation to homelessness administration, we concluded that the sanctioning element of judicial review is very limited. This fact inflates the correlative significance of legal conscientiousness to compliance with administrative law. It is clear that, for compliance to be assured, homelessness decision-makers must apply their legal knowledge to their decision-making tasks. Decision-makers will do this either through fear of sanction, or because they believe it to be the right course of action. The minimal sense in which judicial review may impose sanctions upon such government agencies means, then, that to maximise compliance decision-makers must apply legal knowledge to their work because they believe it be to be the right course of action.

The Incidence of Judicial Review

Legal conscientiousness becomes even more important for homelessness administration when we consider the tiny proportion of decisions which are vulnerable to such sanction. We noted in chapter 1 that Muirfield was the most heavily litigated of the local authorities which took part in the study. It had defended 42 judicial review applications over a period of 14 years. However, we also noted in chapter 1 that it received thousands of homeless applications every year. The volume of final decisions which end up as the subject of judicial review is breathtakingly low. Most administrative decision-making is hidden from scrutiny. This means that the role of 'sanctions' in promoting compliance with administrative law is further minimised.

Complexity of Organisation and the Diffusion of Discretion

There is a further sense, of course, in which homelessness decision-making is hidden from judicial scrutiny. In dealing with the issue of legal knowledge in chapter 2, I argued that due to the complexity of organisations and the fact that often multiple actors have an input into final decision outcomes the requirement that legal knowledge be received by an organisation should be re-framed to mean that it should be received by all those exercising discretion which feeds into the decision outcome. Equally, of course, this applies to the requirement of legal conscientiousness. In order for compliance with administrative law to be maximised, all those contributing to decision outcomes should be concerned to apply their legal knowledge about the lawful exercise of discretion.

This, of course, is an additional reason why legal conscientiousness is crucial to the maximisation of compliance with administrative law. Judicial review isolates the case at hand and artificially reduces it to a single discrete 'decision'. Judicial review, therefore often fails to appreciate the complexities of the administrative process and the multiple uses of discretion which inform the formal decision outcome (Baldwin and McCrudden, 1987: 63). This substantially reduces its potential to directly scrutinise the administrative process as a whole. At best, judicial review scrutinises a tiny proportion of the overall exercise of discretion. This deficit in direct judicial scrutiny also amplifies the importance of legal conscientiousness to compliance with administrative law.

Would Legal Conscientiousness be as Important in Other Contexts?

The above section justified the treatment of legal conscientiousness as an important condition for securing compliance with administrative law in relation to homelessness administration. Does legal conscientiousness carry the same significance in other decision-making contexts?

We observed in chapter 5 that, in general, the sense in which judicial review may operate as a sanction is very limited, particularly when compared with other fields of regulation. However, we also noted that the extent to which judicial review operates as a sanction will vary according to context. Further, in relation to some areas of government decision-making, the propensity to litigate among those disaffected may be greater, and judicial review may then pose a greater threat relative to the number of decisions being made. To use the example of the judicial review of rule-making procedures in the USA, Shapiro (2004) has noted that '[e]ventually legal challenges to nearly every rule became a part of the American political culture.' Such a state of affairs inevitably increases the extent to which judicial review operates as a sanction. If a government agency is facing a litigious population and recognises that judicial scrutiny is a strong possibility, then it will be more likely to comply with the law through fear of enforcement by litigation, and so the need for legal conscientiousness is reduced.

Of course, it is also possible that, even if judicial review does not operate as an external sanction against an agency, compliance with administrative law may be imposed under threat of sanction by senior administrators against junior officers as part of the internal supervision of the bureaucratic process. To this extent, the element of sanction may be introduced from within the administrative agency. A commitment to legality may be generated at a senior level through officers' attitudes, but may be imposed by way of sanction at lower levels. The extent to which this occurs will similarly vary according to organisational context.

The basic argument here is that, even though, generally speaking, judicial review operates as an external sanction in only a limited sense, the extent to which it does so varies according to context. Consequently, the importance of legal conscientiousness to compliance with administrative law also varies. Where the sanction element is particularly low, legal conscientiousness fills the gap and its significance is increased. There is an interplay, in other words, between legal conscientiousness and the sanction element. However, two important points require to be made at this stage. First, legal conscientiousness is still a positive force for compliance with administrative law, even if judicial review operates as a sanction to an increased extent. The argument here is simply that there is a relationship between the two. Secondly, and more importantly, it is difficult to imagine a setting where legal conscientiousness will lose its importance completely. The regulation literature, particularly work on creative compliance, has demonstrated the importance of regulatees' attitude to regulatory compliance. Legal conscientiousness, as we saw in chapter 3, is important for compliance with the spirit, and not just the letter of the law. Further, even where legally conscientious managers impose sanctions for non-compliance with administrative law, systems of internal supervision are likely to leave pockets of discretion unexposed, and so there is always likely to be some role for legal conscientiousness in promoting compliance with administrative law. Legal conscientiousness will always be important, it is suggested, and likely to be very important in many contexts.

Malcolm Feeley (2004), for example, has recently described the considerable success of the courts' attempts to bring about prison reform in the USA. This was achieved through the services of the special master. The special masters were executive assistants of the judge and took control of the implementation process on the judge's behalf, steering through major structural reform. In such a situation where the judge transforms him/herself into an executive agency, actively and deeply involved in the policy-making and implementation processes of the body under scrutiny, the role of legal conscientiousness is substantially reduced. The work of the special masters serve to demonstrate ways in which law has overwhelmed the decision-making environment and asserted its authority in quite dramatic ways. However, even in such situations, some of the prisons were able to combat and resist reform in various ways, and legal conscientiousness, it is suggested, is still an important component in accounting for the varying levels of success in his case studies.

At the beginning of this book I made the caveat that the analytical framework was not equipped to weight the significance of the conditions, relative to each other, to compliance with administrative law. A further observation can be offered now in light of the above discussion. The relative significance of legal conscientiousness to compliance is, to an extent, likely to be context-specific.

Conclusions about Applying the Framework to Other Contexts

The discussion above demonstrates that the importance of legal conscientiousness to the effectiveness of judicial review in securing compliance with administrative law will—at least to some degree—

vary according to the decision-making context. There may also be examples of situations where certain conditions have less pertinence— for instance, the requirement of legal competence in relation to sporadic policy decision-making. However, such questions are a matter for continued enquiry and the framework invites further research to this end. It is important to remember that the framework is not intended to operate as a precise mechanism for assessing the influence of judicial review on government. It operates more as a blunt instrument. Its aim is to offer a foundational research tool which will assist in the complex and painstaking task of assessing the significance of judicial review to government behaviour, through which we may aspire to greater precision.

The main point, however, to be taken from the overall discussion of this section is that the analytical framework, though having emerged from an empirical analysis of homelessness administration, is offered as a framework for general application across all government administration. The significance of legal conscientiousness to compliance with administrative law may vary according to context, but it will always important to some extent. The conditions which make up the analytical framework have been distilled from a particular study of homelessness administration, but relate to the essential elements in the interactions between law and administration.

FUTURE ENQUIRY

Throughout this book, we have repeatedly made the point that the analytical framework is intended to provoke and inform future empirical research. It is perhaps appropriate, then, to end the book by making one additional point about the direction of future enquiry. At the beginning of this chapter we noted that as concern grew about the practical effects of court rulings on government, so did calls for empirical enquiry. This book is, in part, a response to such calls. However, the call for empirical enquiry should, of course, be broader. This thesis helps us think about the relationship between judicial review and government behaviour. As noted, this has become an important concern of administrative law scholars, and the courts have traditionally had an important constitutional role in supervising the activities of government. However, this enquiry is clearly only a small part of the bigger picture of the regulation of government. As our discussion of the decision-making environment in chapter 5 demonstrated, government decision-making is subject to a number of accountability pressures. We still know little about what differences these various pressures make and the complex ways in which decision-makers respond to their broader environment, which includes, but is by no means restricted to, judicial review. Our understanding of government behaviour inevitably leads us to an exploration of the relationship between government action and regulatory supervision. Judicial review is an important part of such regulatory supervision and this book will help us explore it further. But it is only a small part. The next stage of the enquiry is to probe further the empirical relationships between the regulatory regimes and decision-making on the ground.

Bibliography

ADLER, M (forthcoming) 'A Socio-Legal Approach to Adminstrative Justice' *Law & Policy*.
—— and HENMAN, P (2001) 'e-Justice: A Comparative Study of Computerisation and Procedural Justice in Social Security' *International Review of Law, Computers and Technology*, vol 15, 195.
—— and LONGHURST, B (1994) *Discourse, Power and Justice: Towards a New Sociology of Imprisonment* (Routledge, London).
AIRO-FARULLA, G (2001) 'Rationality and Judicial Review of Administrative Action' *Melbourne University Law Review*, vol 24, 543.
ALLEN, TRS (2003) 'Doctrine and Theory in Administrative Law: An Elusive Quest for the Limits of Jurisdiction' *Public Law*, 429.
ARDEN, A and HUNTER, C (2002) *Homelessness and Allocations* (Legal Action Group, London).
AYRES, I and BRAITHWAITE, J (1992) *Responsive Regulation: Transcending the Deregulation Debate* (Oxford University Press, Oxford).
BALDWIN, R (1995) *Rules and Government* (Oxford University Press, Oxford).
—— and CAVE, M (1999) *Understanding Regulation* (Oxford University Press, Oxford).
—— and McCRUDDEN, C (1987) *Regulation and Public Law* (London, Weidenfeld and Nicolson).
—— SCOTT, C and HOOD, C (1998) *A Reader on Regulation* (Oxford University Press, Oxford).
BARBER, N (2001) 'Prelude to the Separation of Powers' *Cambridge Law Journal*, vol 60, 59.
BARDACH, E and KAGAN, R (1982) *Going by the Book: the Problem of Regulatory Unreasonableness* (Temple University Press, Philadelphia).
BARON, A and SCOTT, C (1992) 'The Citizen's Charter Programme' *Modern Law Review*, vol 55, 526.
BEATSON, J (1984) 'The Scope of Judicial Review for Error of Law' *Oxford Journal of Legal Studies*, vol 4, 22.
BERTHOUD, R and BRYSON, A (1997) 'Social security appeals: what do the claimants want?' 4 *Journal of Social Security Law* 17.
BLACK, J (1997) *Rules and Regulators* (Clarendon Press, Oxford).
—— (1998) 'Talking About Regulation' [1998] *Public Law* 77.
BRAITHWAITE, J (1985) *To Punish or Persuade: Enforcement of Coal Mine Safety* (State University of New York Press, Albany).

BRAITHWAITE, J (2002) 'Rules and Principles: A Theory of Legal Certainty' *Australian Journal of Legal Philosophy*, vol 27, 47.

BRIDGES, L, GAME, C, LOMAS, N, MCBRIDE, J and RANSOM, S (1987) *Legality and Local Politics* (Avebury, Aldershot).

BRIDGES, L, MESZAROS, G and SUNKIN, M (1996) *Judicial Review in Perspective* (Cavendish Press, London).

—— (2000) 'Regulating the Judicial Review Case Load' *Public Law* 651.

BUCK, T (1998) 'Judicial Review and the Discretionary Social Fund' in T Buck (ed), *Judicial Review and Social Welfare* (Printer, London).

CANE, P (*forthcoming*) 'Administrative Law as Regulation' in C Parker, J Braithwaite, C Scott and N Lacey (eds), *Regulating Law* (Oxford University Press, Oxford).

—— (2004) 'Understanding Judicial Review and its Impact' in M Hertogh and S Halliday (eds), *Judicial Review and Bureaucratic Impact* (Cambridge University Press, Cambridge).

CANON, B (2004) 'Studying Bureaucratic Implementation of Judicial Policies in the US: Conceptual and Methodological Approaches' in M Hertogh and S Halliday (eds), *Judicial Review and Bureaucratic Impact* (Cambridge University Press, Cambridge).

CICOUREL, A (1968) *The Social Organization of Juvenile Justice* (John Wiley & Sons, New York).

CLYDE, JJ and EDWARDS, DJ (2000) *Judicial Review* (W Green, Edinburgh).

COGLIANESE, C (2002) 'Empirical Analysis and Administrative Law' *University of Illinois Law Review*, 1111.

COHEN, S (2001) *States of Denial: Knowing About Atrocities and Suffering* (Polity Press, Cambridge).

COLLINS, H (1999) *Regulating Contracts* (Oxford University Press, Oxford).

COOPER, D (1995) 'Local Government Legal Consciousness in the Shadow of Juridification' *Journal of Law & Society*, vol 22, 506.

COWAN, D (1997) *Homelessness: The (In)Appropriate Applicant* (Ashgate/Dartmouth, Aldershot).

—— (2003) ' "Rage at Westsinster": Socio-Legal Reflections on the Power of Sale' *Social & Legal Studies*, vol 12, 177.

COWAN, D and HALLIDAY, S (2003) *The Appeal of Internal Review: Law, Administrative Justice and the (Non-)Emergence of Disputes* (Hart Publishing, Oxford).

CRAIG, P (1993) 'Procedures and Administrative Decision-Making: A Common Law Perspective' *European Review of Public Law*, 55.

—— (2003) *Administrative Law*, 5th ed (Sweet & Maxwell, London).

CRANSTON, R (1994) 'Reviewing Judicial Review' in G Richardson and H Genn (eds), *Administrative Law and Government Action* (Oxford University Press, Oxford).

CREYKE, R and MCMILLAN, J (2002) 'Executive Perceptions of Administrative Law—An Empirical Study' *Australian Journal of Administrative Law*, vol 9, 163.

—— (2004) 'The Operation of Judicial Review in Australia' in Hertogh, M and Halliday, S (eds) *Judicial Review and Bureaucratic Impact* (Cambridge University Press, Cambridge).

DAINTITH, T and PAGE, A (1999) *The Executive in the Constitution: Structure, Autonomy, and Internal Control* (Oxford University Press, Oxford).

DAVIS, KC (1969) *Discretionary Justice: A Preliminary Enquiry* (Baton Rouge, Louisiana State University Press).

DE SMITH, SA, WOOLF, H and JOWELL, J (1995) *Judicial Review of Administrative Action* (London, Sweet & Maxwell).

DEPARTMENT OF THE ENVIRONMENT (1991) *Code of Guidance on Homelessness* (3rd ed) (HMSO, London).

DALLEY, G, and BERTHOUD, R (1992) *Challenging Discretion: The Social Fund Review Procedure* (Policy Studies Institute, London).

DOTAN, Y, (1999) 'Judicial Rhetoric, Government Lawyers, and Human Rights: The Case of the Israeli High Court of Justice during the Intifada' *Law & Society Review*, vol 33, no. 2, 319.

—— (2004) 'Legalizing the Unlegalizeable: Terrorism, Secret Services and Judicial Review in Israel 1970–2001' in M Hertogh and S Halliday (eds), *Judicial Review and Bureaucratic Impact* (Cambridge University Press, Cambridge).

DREWRY, G (2000) 'The New Public Management' in J Jowell and D Oliver, *The Changing Constitution*, 4th ed (Oxford University Press, Oxford).

EMERSON, R (1983) 'Holistic Effects in Social Control Decision-Making', *Law & Society Review*, vol 17, 425.

—— FRETZ, R and SHAW, L (1995) *Writing Ethnographic Fieldnotes* (University of Chicago Press, Chicago).

—— and PALEY, B (1992) 'Organizational Horizons and Complaint-Filing' in K Hawkins (ed), *The Uses of Discretion* (Clarendon Press, Oxford).

ENDICOTT, T (1998) 'Questions of Law' *Law Quarterly Review*, vol 114, 292.

FEELEY, M (1992) 'Hollow Hopes, Flypaper, and Metaphors' *Law and Social Inquiry*, vol 17, 745.

—— (2004) 'Implementing Court Orders: Judges as Executives' in M Hertogh and S Halliday (eds), *Judicial Review and Bureaucratic Impact* (Cambridge University Press, Cambridge).

—— and RUBIN, E (1998) *Judicial Policy Making and the Modern State: How the Courts Reformed America's Prisons* (Cambridge, Cambridge University Press).

FISH, S (1989) *Doing What Comes Naturally: Change, Rhetoric, and the Practice of Theory in Literary and Legal Studies* (Oxford University Press, Oxford).

FISHER, E and SCHMIDT, P (2001) 'Seeing the "Blind Spots" in Administrative Law: Theory, Practice, and Rulemaking Settlements in the United States' *Common Law World Review*, vol 30, 348.

GALLIGAN, D (1976) 'The Nature and Function of Policies within Discretionary Power' *Public Law*, 332.

—— (1986) *Discretionary Powers: A Legal Study of Official Discretion* (Clarendon Press, Oxford).

—— (1996) *Due Process and Fair Procedures: A Study of Administrative Procedures* (Clarendon Press, Oxford).

—— (2001) 'Authoritarianism in Government and Administration: The Promise of Administrative Justice' *Current Legal Problems*, vol 54, 79.

GENN, H (1994) 'Tribunal review of administrative decision-making' in Richardson G and Genn, H *Administrative Law and Government Action* (Clarendon Press, Oxford).

—— (1999) *Paths to Justice: What People Do and Think About Going to Law* (Hart Publishling, Oxford).

—— and PATERSON, A (2001) *Paths to Justice Scotland: What People in Scotland Do and Think About Going to Law* (Hart Publishing, Oxford).

GRABOSKY, P and BRAITHWAITE, J (1986) *Of Manners Gentle: Enforcement Strategies of Australian Business Regulatory Agencies* (Oxford University Press, Melbourne).

HADFIELD, B and WEAVER, E (1995) 'Judicial Review in Perspective: An Investigation of Trends in the Use and Operation of the Judicial Review Procedure in Northern Ireland' *Northern Ireland Legal Quarterly*, vol 46, 113.

HALL, C, SCOTT, C and HOOD, C (2000) *Telecommunications Regulation: Culture, Chaos and Interdependence Inside The Regulatory Process* (Routledge, London).

HALLIDAY, S (1996) 'Homelessness Law and the Physically Disabled' *Juridical Review*, vol 6, 374.

—— (1998) 'Researching the 'impact' of judicial review on routine administrative decision-making', in D Cowan (ed), *Housing: Participation and Exclusion* (Dartmouth, Aldershot).

—— (2000a) 'The influence of judicial review on bureaucratic decision-making' *Public Law*, 110.

—— (2000b) 'Institutional Racism in Bureaucratic Decision-Making: A Case Study in the Administration of Homelessness Law' *Journal of Law & Society*, vol 27, 449.

HAMMOND, A (1998) 'Judicial Review: the continuing interplay between law and policy' *Public Law*, 34.

HANCHER, L and MORAN, M (1989) 'Organising Regulatory Space' in L Hancher and M Moran (eds), *Capitalism, Culture, and Economic Regulation* (Clarendon Press, Oxford).

HANDLER, J (1986) *The Conditions of Discretion: Autonomy, Community, Bureaucracy* (Russell Sage Foundation, New York).

HARLOW, C (1976) 'Administrative Reaction to Judicial Review', *Public Law*, 116.

HARLOW, C and RAWLINGS, R (1992) *Pressure Through Law* (Routledge, London).
—— (1997) *Law and Administration*, 2nd ed (Butterworths, London).
HARRIS, M and PARTINGTON, M (1999) 'Introduction' in M Harris and M Partington (eds), *Administrative Justice in the 21st Century* (Hart Publishing, Oxford).
HAWKINS, K (1984) *Environment and Enforcement* (Oxford University Press, Oxford).
—— (1990) 'Compliance Strategy, Prosecution Policy and Aunt Sally' *British Journal of Criminology*, vol 30, 444.
—— (1992) 'The Use of Legal Discretion: Perspectives from Law and Social Science' in Hawkins, K (ed) *The Uses of Discretion* (Clarendon Press, Oxford).
—— (2002) *Law as Last Resort: Prosecution Decision-Making in a Regulatory Agency* (Oxford University Press, Oxford).
HERTOGH, M (2001) 'Coercion, Cooperation, and Control: Understanding the Policy Impact of Administrative Courts and the Ombudsman in the Netherlands' *Law & Policy*, vol 23, 47.
—— and HALLIDAY, S (2004) 'Judicial Review and Bureaucratic Impact in Future Research' in M Hertogh and S Halliday (eds), *Judicial Review and Bureaucratic Impact* (Cambridge University Press, Cambridge).
HOOD, C (1990) 'A Public Management for All Seasons?' *Public Administration*, vol 69, 3.
—— SCOTT, C, JAMES, O, JONES, G and TRAVERS, T (1999) *Regulation Inside Government: Waste-Watchers, Quality Police, and Sleeze-Busters* (Oxford University Press, Oxford).
HUTTER, B (1997) *Compliance: Regulation and Environment* (Clarendon Press, Oxford).
ISON, T (1999) 'Administrative Justice: Is it Such a Good Idea?' in M Harris and M Partington (eds), *Administrative Justice in the 21st Century* (Hart Publishing, Oxford).
JAMES, S (1996) 'The Political and Administrative Consequences of Judicial Review' *Public Administration*, vol 74, 613.
JEWELL, C (2003) *Responding to Need in the 'Three Worlds of Social Welfare': How Welfare State Traditions and Social Service Organizations Impact the Role Caseworkers Play in Shaping Welfare Policy in the United States, Germany and Sweden* (unpublished PhD dissertation, University of California, Berkeley).
JOWELL, J and LESTER, A (1988) 'Proportionality: Neither Novel nor Dangerous' in J Jowel and D Oliver (eds), *New Directions in Judicial Review* (Stevens and Sons, London).
JONES, T (1989) 'Administrative Law, Regulation, and Legitimacy' *Journal of Law and Society*, vol 16, 410.
KAGAN, R (1978) *Regulatory Justice: Implementing a Wage-Price Freeze* (Russell Sage Foundation, New York).

KAGAN, R, GUNNINGHAM, N and THORNTON, D (2003) 'Explaining Corporate Environmental Performance: How Does Regulation Matter?' *Law & Society Review*, vol 37, 51.

—— and SCHOLZ, J (1984) 'The "Criminology of the Corporation" and Regulatory Enforcement Strategies' in K Hawkins and J Thomas (eds), *Enforcing Regulation* (Kluwer-Nijhoff, Boston, Mass.).

KERRY, Sir M (1986) 'Administrative law and judicial review—the practical effects of developments over the past 25 years on administration in central government' *Public Administration*, vol 64, 163.

LEMPERT, R (1992) 'Discretion in a Behavioural Perspective' in K Hawkins (ed), *The Uses of Discretion* (Clarendon Press, Oxford).

LIND, A and TYLER, T (1988) *The Social Psychology of Procedural Justice* (Plenum, New York).

LIPSKY, M (1980) *Street-Level Bureaucracry: Dilemmas of the Individual in Public Services* (Russell Sage Foundation, New York).

LIVINGSTONE, S (1995) 'The Impact of Judicial Review on Prisons' in B Hadfield (ed), *Judicial Review: A Thematic Approach* (Gill and MacMillan, Dublin).

LOVELAND, I (1995) *Housing Homeless Persons* (Clarendon Press, Oxford).

LOUGHLIN, M and QUINN, PM (1993) 'Prisons, Rules and Courts: A Study in Administrative Law' *Modern Law Review*, vol 56, 497.

McBARNET, D and WHELAN, C (1991) 'The Elusive Spirit of the Law: Formalism and the Struggle for Legal Control' *Modern Law Review*, vol 54, 848.

McCANN, M (1992) 'Reform Litigation on Trial' *Law and Social Inquiry*, vol 17, 715.

—— (1994) *Rights at Work: Pay Equity Reform and the Politics of Legal Mobilization* (University of Chicago Press, London).

MASHAW, J (1983) *Bureaucratic Justice: Managing Social Security Disability Claims* (Yale University Press, New Haven).

MULCAHY, L (1999) 'Sliding Scales of Justice at the end of the Century—A Cause for Complaints' in M Harris and M Partington (eds), *Administrative Justice in the 21st Century* (Hart Publishing, Oxford).

MULLAN, D (1975) 'Fairness: the New Natural Justice?' *University of Toronto Law Journal*, 25, 281.

MULLEN, T, PICK, K and PROSSER, T (1996) *Judicial Review in Scotland* (John Wiley & Sons, Chichester).

NONET, P (1969) *Administrative Justice* (Russell Sage Foundation, New York).

OBADINA, D (1988), *The Impact of Judicial Review on Local Authority Decision-Making*, unpublished PhD Thesis (University of Wales, Cardiff).

—— (1998) 'Judicial Review and Gypsy Site Provision' in T Buck (ed), *Judicial Review and Social Welfare* (Printer, London).

PAGE, A (1999) 'The Citizen's Charter and Administrative Justice' in M Harris and M Partington (eds), *Administrative Justice in the 21st Century* (Hart Publishing, Oxford).

PARKER, C (1999a) 'Compliance Professionalism and Regulatory Community: The Australian Trade Practices Regime' *Journal of Law and Society*, vol 26, 215.

—— (1999b) 'How to Win Hearts and Minds: Corporate Compliance Policies for Sexual Harassment' *Law and Policy*, vol 21, 21.

PEARCE, F and TOMBS, S (1990) 'Ideology, Hegemony, and Empiricism: Compliance Theories of Regulation' *British Journal of Criminology*, vol 30, 423.

POLLARD, D (1998) 'Judicial Review and Homelessness' in T Buck (ed), *Judicial Review and Social Welfare* (Printer, London).

POWER, M (1997) *The Audit Society: Rituals of Verification* (Oxford University Press, Oxford).

PROSSER, T (1983) *Test Cases for the Poor* (Child Poverty Action Group, London).

RAWLINGS, R. (1986) 'Judicial Review and the "Control of Government" ' *Public Administration*, vol 64, 135.

RICHARDSON, G (2004) 'Impact Studies in the UK' in M Hertogh and S Halliday (eds), *Judicial Review and Bureaucratic Impact* (Cambridge University Press, Cambridge).

—— (1993) *Law, Process and Custody: Prisoners and Patients* (Weidenfield & Nicolson, London).

—— and MACHIN, D (2000) 'Judicial Review and Tribunal Decision-Making: A Study of the Mental Health Review Tribunal' *Public Law*, 494.

—— OGUS, A and BURROWS, P (1983) *Policing Pollution: A Study of Regulation and Enforcement* (Clarendon Press, Oxford).

—— and SUNKIN, M (1996) 'Judicial Review: Questions of Impact' *Public Law*, 79.

ROBSON, P and POUSTIE, M (1996) *Homeless Persons and the Law* (Butterworths, London).

—— and WATCHMAN, PQ (1981) 'The Homeless Persons Obstacle Race' *Journal of Social Welfare Law* 1 and 65.

ROSENBERG, G (1991) *The Hollow Hope: Can Courts Bring About Social Change?* (University of Chicago Press, London).

—— (1996) 'Positivism, Interpretivism, and the Study of Law' *Law and Social Inquiry*, vol 21, 435.

SAINSBURY, R and EARDLEY, T (1991) *Housing Benefit Reviews* (HMSO, London).

—— HIRST, M and LAWTON, D (1995) *Evaluation of Disability Living Allowance and Attendance Allowance*, Department of Social Security Research Report No 41 (HMSO, London).

SCHULTZ, D (ed) 1998 *Leveraging the Law: Using the Courts to Achieve Social Change* (Peter Lang, New York).

—— and GOTTLIEB, SE (1998) 'Legal Functionalism and Social Change: A Reassessment of Rosenberg's *The Hollow Hope*' in D Schultz (ed),

Leveraging the Law: Using the Courts to Achieve Social Change (Peter Lang, New York).

SCHUTZ, A (1967) *The Phenomenology of the Social World* (Northwestern University Press, Evanston).

SCOTT, C (2000) 'Accountability in the Regulatory State' *Journal of Law & Society*, vol 27, 38.

SENEVIRATNE, M (2002) *Ombudsmen: Public Services and Administrative Justice* (Butterworths, London).

SHAPIRO, M (2004) 'Judicial Review and Bureaucratic Impact: The Future of EU Administrative Law' in M Hertogh and S Halliday (eds), *Judicial Review and Bureaucratic Impact* (Cambridge University Press, Cambridge).

—— and STONE SWEET, A (2002) *On Law, Politics and Judicialisation* (Oxford University Press, Oxford).

SOSSIN, L (1994) 'Redistributing Democracy: Authority, Discretion and the Possibility of Engagement in the Welfare State' 26 *Ottawa Law Review*, 1.

—— (2004) 'The Politics of Soft Law: How Judicial Decisions Influence Bureaucratic Discretion in Canada' in M Hertogh and S Halliday (eds), *Judicial Review and Bureaucratic Impact* (Cambridge University Press, Cambridge).

STONE SWEET, A (2000) *Governing with Judges: Constitutional Politics in Europe* (Oxford, Oxford University Press).

SUNKIN, M (2004) 'Conceptual Issues in Researching the Impact of Judicial Review on Government Bureaucracies' in M Hertogh and S Halliday (eds), *Judicial Review and Bureaucratic Impact* (Cambridge University Press, Cambridge).

—— and LE SUEUR, AP (1991) 'Can Government Control Judicial Review?', vol 44 *Current Legal Problems*, 161.

—— PICK, K (2001) 'The Changing Impact of Judicial Review: The Independent Review Service of the Social Fund' [2001] *Public Law*, 736.

THOMAS, R (2003) 'The Impact of Judicial Review on Asylum' *Public Law*, 479.

TOMKINS, A (2003) *Public Law* (Oxford University Press, Oxford).

TREASURY SOLICITOR'S DEPARTMENT (1995) *Judge Over Your Shoulder. Judicial Review: Balancing the Scales* (Cabinet Office, London).

TYLER, T (1988) 'What is procedural justice?' 22 *Law & Society Review* 103.

VINCENT-JONES, P (2000) 'Central-Local Relations under the Local Government Act 1999: A New Consensus?' *Modern Law Review*, vol 63, 84.

—— (2002) 'Values and Purpose in Government: Central-local Relations in Regulatory Perspective' *Journal of Law and Society*, vol 29, 27.

WADE, HWR and FORSYTH, CF (2000) *Administrative Law*, 8th ed (Oxford University Press, Oxford).

WAEGEL, WB (1981) 'Case Routinization in Investigative Police Work' *Social Problems* vol 28, 263.

YEUNG, K (2004) *Securing Compliance: A Principled Approach* (Hart Publishing, Oxford).

Index

accountability pressures *see* financial
    management
Adler, M 120–4
administration
    good 13–14
    homelessness, and legal conscientious-
        ness 169–73
administrative efficiency 148–9
administrative justice 111–12, 156–8
    activities covered 114
    administrative legality and 113–14
    bureaucratic rationality 117, 122
    competing models 127
    conceptions 116–25
    consumerism 120–1, 123–4
    ideal types 120–1, 122–4
    managerialism 120, 122
    marketisation 121, 122
    Mashaw's models 116–18
    moral judgment 118–19, 122
    professional treatment 118, 119–20,
        122
    scholarship 113–15
administrative law 165–6
    definition 8, 111
    judicial review and 161–2
    overview of doctrine 128–30
    regulatory goal 12–14
    research on impact 6
    review
        goals 129
        grounds 129–30, 138
        spirit v letter 80
agency autonomy *see* judicial control
amoral calculators 163
analytical framework 166–8
applicants, bogus, pre-empting tactics
    64–5
application questions 140–1
axiomatic decision-making 54

Baldwin, R 11, 39
Bardach, E 53
Best Value regimes 94

Black, Julia 72–3, 74
bogus applicants, pre-empting tactics
    64–5
bureaucratic rationality 117, 122

Cane, P 7, 12
Canon, B 71
Citizen's Charter 121, 122
Collins, H 11
common law 112, 164, 165
compliance behaviour, continuums
    164–6
compliance focus, limits 9
Compulsory Competitive Tendering 94
conscientiousness *see* legal conscientious-
    ness
consideration of relevant facts, rules 130
consumerism 120–1, 123–4
corporations, typology 163
Cowan, D 55, 94, 99
creative compliance 60–9
    see also legal conscientiousness
    definition 62–3
    faith in law, lack 60–1
    legal control, avoidance 61–5
Creyke, R 7
criminology of the corporation *see* corpo-
    rations, typology
culture of suspicion 55–9

Daintith, T 46, 61, 96
decision-making
    axiomatic 54
    compliance conditions 164–5
    environment 87–8, 106–8
        compliance conditions 165
        financial management 89–93
        flexibility 106
        law's strength, conditioning factors
        101–6
        normative systems 88–9
        performance audit 94–6
        persuasion 105
        political pressure 96–9

decision-making (*cont.*):
  environment (*cont.*):
    sanctions 103–5
    social/political pressures 99–101
  outcomes, substantive rationality
      132–7
  process
    rationality 142–3
      administrative law principles 150
      administrative policies 150–3
      relevant and irrelevant facts 153–6
  typologies of decision-makers 162–3
delegation of decision-making, rule 129
discretion
  fettering, rule 129
  legal conscientiousness 171
disproportionality *see* proportionality
    doctrine

Eastbank HPU 26–8
  axiomatic decision-making 54
  culture of suspicion 56–8
  intentionality panel 46–9
  legal knowledge 81–2
  social/political pressures (case study)
      100–1
  temporary accommodation pressures
      (case study) 89–93
efficiency *see* administrative efficiency
Emerson, R 20
error of law 129, 137–42
  application questions 140–1
  fact and law questions 139–42
  jurisdiction 138

fact and law questions 139–42
fact-finding, statutory requirements
      142–3
faith in law, lack 60–1
Feeley, Malcolm 173
fettering of discretion, rule 129
financial management 89–93
flexibility 106

Galligan, D 6–7, 53, 104, 149, 157
Genn, H 104
good administration 13–14
government agencies, definition 3n

Harlow, C 8, 122, 145
Harris, M 114
Hawkins, Keith 40, 54, 99–100
Hertogh, M 60, 73

heuristic device
  individual conditions 17–18
  optimal compliance, level 16–17
  perfect compliance as regulatory goal
      17
  questions of degree 18–19
homeless persons units (HPUs) 21–8
homelessness 29–30
  administration and legal conscientious-
      ness 169–73
  intentionality 30
  law 28–31
  legislative changes 31
  local connection 30–1 ·
  political antipathy (case study) 97–9
  priority need 30
  soft law 39–40
Hood, C 88
HPUs *see* homeless persons units

impact research 6
incompetent organisations 163
intentionality
  homelessness 30
  panel 46–9
interpretation of law 71–2, 82–3
  interpretive communities 72–3
  interpretivism 10
intuition *see* professional intuition
irrationality *see* Wednesbury unreason-
      ableness

judicial control, agency autonomy and
      130–1
  rationality of decision-making 132–7,
      142–3
judicial impact 9
judicial review, functions 15–16
jurisdiction 138
justice *see* administrative justice

Kagan, R 39, 53, 158, 162–3
knowledge *see* legal knowledge

legal advisors, organisational relation-
      ships 50–1
legal competence *see* interpretation of
      law
legal conscientiousness 53–4, 68–9
  see also creative compliance
  contexts 169, 171–4
  culture of suspicion 55–9
  diffusion of discretion 171

homelessness administration and
169–73
judicial review and 170–1
legal knowledge 65–8
organisational complexity 171
professional intuition 54–5
role of sanctions 170
legal control, avoidance 61–5
abuse of legal process 61–2
bullet proofing decisions 63–4
pre-empting creative tactics 64–5
legal knowledge
see also interpretation of law
application
bounded 80–2
bureaucratic 74–80
barriers 46–51
Eastbank HPU 81–2
legal conscientiousness 65–8
Muirfield HPU 45–6
organisational complexity 41–6,
46–9
reception 39–41
relationships with legal advisors 50–1
Timbergreens (case study) 74–80, 81–2
Lipsky, M 59, 100
local authorities *see* homeless persons
units
local political antipathy towards homeless (case study) 97–9
Loveland, I 40, 54–5, 93

McBarnet, D 62–3, 80
McCann, M 9–10
managerialism 120, 122
marketisation 121, 122
Mashaw, J 108, 124, 149, 157
developments on models 119–24
models of administrative justice
116–18
methodological divide 9–10
moral judgment 118–19, 122
Muirfield HPU 25–6
assessments and advice team 43–4
casework team 42–3
culture of suspicion 59
legal conscientiousness 66–8
performance related pay (case study)
94–6
political antipathy towards homeless
(case study) 97–9
reception of legal knowledge 45–6
sanctions 103–4

structure and operations 41–5
temporary accommodation team
44–5
Mullen, D 7

national security 149–50
New Public Management 121

organisational complexity, legal knowledge 41–6

Parker, C 39, 73
performance audit 94, 96
performance related pay (case study)
94–6
persuasion 105
political citizens 163
political pressure 96–9
antipathy towards homeless (case
study) 97–9
remote pressures 99–101
positivism 10
Power, Michael 94
procedural fairness 143–7
adminstrative efficiency 148–9
national security 149–50
professional intuition 54–5
professional treatment 118, 119–20,
122
proportionality doctrine 130, 136–7

questions
of application 140–1
of fact and law 139–42

reasonableness *see Wednesbury* unreasonableness
regulatees *see* decision-makers
regulatory perspective
administrative law 12–14
perfect compliance 17
regulation, definition 10–11
regulatory goals 11–12
two levels 14–15
relational distance 72–3
relevant and irrelevant facts 130,
153–6
research
administrative law 6
approach 19–20
choice of local authorities 21–3
judicial review 5
techniques 20–1

Richardson, G 106
Rosenburg, Gerald 9–10

sanctions, role 170
scope of enquiry 6–8
Scott, Colin 88
security *see* national security
Shapiro, M 172
social/political pressures 99–101, 174–5
soft law 39–40
Sossin, L 39–40, 72
Sunkin, M 63, 73, 166
suspicion, culture 55–9

temporary accommodation pressures
        (case study) 89–93
    decision-making practices 91–3

policy initiatives 90–1
Timbergreens' HPU 23–5
    culture of suspicion 56, 58
    legal control, avoidance 61–2, 64
    legal knowledge, bureaucratic applica-
        tion (case study) 74–80, 81–2
    pre-empting creative tactics 65
Tomkins, A 11

ultra vires doctrine 129
unreasonableness *see* Wednesbury
        unreasonableness

Vincent-Jones, P 12–13

Wednesbury unreasonableness 130,
        132–6, 153, 158